For teaching me about health and caring for people

To Dr. Crowe: thank you for healing me and introducing me to my life's work. My gratitude is also extended to the many NUCCA instructors who have shown me how to achieve the level of corrections necessary to heal people. Thank you, Dr. Tom Owen and the AMC family for helping to make our clinic a haven for the sick.

For true healing

In 1992 my life was changed forever when I discovered who God really is. Actually, it was really God who reached out to me and put me on the path of truth, health and life. I have experienced an amazing journey ever since. A well-known doctor once said, "Don't forget where the healing comes from." I am eternally grateful that I understand what these words mean.

Important Note

This book is not intended as a substitute for
the medical recommendation of your doctor
or other healthcare providers. Rather, it is
intended to offer information to help the reader
to partner with physicians, health professionals
and spiritual counselors in a mutual quest for
optimum health and wholeness.

I'm Sick and Tired of Being Sick and Tired

SIX KEYS

(to)

Health

and

Wholeness

■ ■ ■ ■ ■

Dr.
Kerry Johnson

VMI PUBLISHERS
Partnering With Christian Authors, Publishing Christian and Inspirational Books
Sisters, OR

Published by

VMI PUBLISHERS

Partnering With Christian Authors, Publishing Christian and Inspirational Books

a division of VMI Publishers
Sisters, Oregon
www.vmipublishers.com

ISBN: 1-933204-27-3

Library of Congress Control Number: 2006929964

Author Contact: www.sixkeystohealth.com

Table of Contents

How Healthy Are We   11
What Is Health?   15

Part I

The "Whole" Body   21
Body Balance   29
Nutrition   61
Exercise   93
Rest   101
Positive Mental Attitude   109

Part II

Mind & Spirit - Which Worldview?   117
Body, Soul & Spirit - The Perfect Design   135
A Case of the Tail Wagging the Dog!   141
Mission Impossible?   145
The Connection!   153
Can I Get a Witness?   157

Epilogue - How I Ate the Elephant   167
Glossary   169
References   170

Acknowledgements

For making this book a reality

I would like to begin by expressing my gratitude to Bill Carmichael and the awesome team at VMI Publishers for making this book so much better than I could have on my own. I would especially like to thank my editor, Colleen Wilson, for helping this doctor to become a writer. For my sister Sheri, English teacher extraordinaire, who made the manuscript presentable in the first place, my love and thanks! I am also grateful for Drs. Bruntjen and Leach along with the rest of the staff at Johnson Chiropractic, P.A. who graciously cared for my patients during the ten weeks I was away to write.

For walking beside me

Without question, you would not be reading this now if it were not for a few people who have walked with me on my journey towards health. To Mom and Dad, thanks for your love, patience and never ending support and for your example of staying the course. To my wife Lisa: words can't describe my gratefulness for the grace, love and unending encouragement you lavish on me. I am truly blessed! To Matt and Beth, thank you for making parenting so easy.

For teaching me about spiritual matters

To Don and Marion: thank you for introducing me to Cursillo. To the pastors who have served as mentors throughout my spiritual journey: Pat Hall, Mark Opseth, Jim Sky, Rick Moe and Kraig Kestner; I am grateful for the investment of time, knowledge and love you have shared with me.

Introduction

I intend to provide you with an opportunity to discover knowledge that will lead you to experience true health. Your success will most likely depend on three key factors: A willingness to overcome preconceived ideas, sufficient desire to accept the truth, and sensitivity to receiving what I call "Aha Moments." These are times when the light bulb suddenly turns on, and your intuition delivers to your consciousness a truth you have not previously understood. You might find yourself saying something like "I get it!" or "That makes sense!" or "I never knew that!" The bigger the revelation, the more apt you are to apply the new truth and thus change whatever it is that is keeping you from being healthy. Allow me to illustrate this principle.

Fishing is one of my favorite pastimes. I especially love to fish for the Walleyed Pike, the official state fish of Minnesota where I live. The Walleye is very finicky, elusive and sometimes very difficult to catch. To further the challenge, I have recently fished in some Walleye tournaments. I consider myself to be a good Walleye fisherman, having done so since I was a five year-old child from the front of my dad's boat. The best Walleye fishermen will tell you the two keys to success are location and presentation. In other words, you have to be where the fish are, and you have to present the proper lure to the fish in the proper manner.

Recently, a friend and I entered a Walleye tournament on a lake I have fished regularly for the past ten years. I know what type and color of lures the Walleye in this lake like best. We spent two days pre-fishing the tournament and found just the right spot where we believed we would catch some big fish. On the first day of the tournament, we caught only one walleye, which was not too good at weigh-in time when we were suppose to have six big fish (in these tournaments all fish caught are kept alive and released after the weigh-in).

To make matters worse, the two men in a boat right next to us were catching nice big fish. They were so close I could see what they were using for lures and bait. I scratched my head, knowing they had the wrong lure for this lake. Out of frustration, I switched to a similar lure but with the color I knew the fish preferred. Yet we still failed to catch fish. The next day however, we switched lures again and caught six nice fish! We nearly won the prize for the best improvement from day one to day two. (This same catch the day before would have placed us high enough in the tournament to win prize money.)

My stubborn preconceived notions about the best lures and colors to fish with kept us from switching our presentation soon enough to be successful in the tournament. The "Aha Moment" came the evening of that first day. My friend and I couldn't deny the truth that the men in the boat next to us had caught fish. We were so moved by this fact we decided to match their same exact color of lure and presentation, which is what brought us success the second day. We couldn't deny what worked because we saw the results with our own eyes. We discovered a new truth and applied it.

Another event in my life highlights this same principle. I am a Doctor of Chiropractic. In my early years of practice, our clinic always took a financial dip during the month of June. I had developed several preconceived notions as to why. Ideas such as: People were healthier in the summer because they were more active; school was out so everyone was on vacation; people were more concerned about getting to the cabin, going fishing, and their summer recreation than their health during the few precious summer months in Minnesota. Armed with these and other excuses, we simply braced ourselves for a bad June every year.

One April weekend I was at a practice development seminar in Phoenix, AZ. The speaker brought up this same subject and one of his statements became an "Aha Moment" for me. He said, "Doctors, you are responsible for the success or failure of your practice. If you have a bad month it's not the weather, your receptionist or any other factor. You alone are to blame!" I made a decision then and there to take full responsibility for my practice. My first goal was to prevent the June financial slump. Guess what? We set a practice record that June for gross receipts and number of new patients seen!

My own preconceived ideas had caused my practice problems. My sensitivity to recognize the "Aha Moment," along with my willingness to overcome my preconceived ideas, and a desire to apply a new truth about building a successful practice has brought me great success. A mentor in my profession has shared the following saying:

> *"If I always do what I have always done,*
> *I will always get what I have always got."*

Another saying made famous by Albert Einstein reads:

> *"Insanity: Doing the same thing over and*
> *over again and expecting different results."*

Both of these sayings have stuck with me over the years and have motivated me to move out of my comfort zone to make positive changes in my own life. We are creatures of habit, but true changes for the better usually come when our mind is open to receiving concepts that may go against our attitudes and preconceived ideas. Much of our faulty thinking affecting our attitudes and behavior is based on childhood perceptions and negative experiences that actually have little basis in truth. I remember an old friend from Tennessee used to call it *"stinkin thinkin."* How many people believe they are stupid, ugly, clumsy, bad, undeserving, or worthless, because a loved one, a friend, or a teacher told them so during an impressionable age?

 *This sign appears in several places throughout the book. It will alert you to areas where you may need to take extra precaution not to let your preconceived ideas prevent you from experiencing an "Aha Moment."*

This is a book about common sense. I am trusting as you read you will say to yourself, "This makes sense." This book has been a labor of love for me because I have dedicated my life to helping people achieve lasting health and, along the way, finding it myself. My prayer for you is that you will be able to read this book with an open mind. Please don't allow your preconceived ideas about yourself, others, and what you think you know about health prevent you from experiencing some "Aha Moments!" sufficient enough to improve your life. —

DR. KERRY L. JOHNSON

CHAPTER ONE

How Healthy
Are We?

America is becoming health conscious. As millions of baby boomers begin to reach retirement age, health is becoming a major issue. Besides the weather, can you think of a more common topic for casual conversation than health? As a society, we're not just talking about health, we are spending billions in our attempts to reclaim it. Today, roughly 15 % of the gross national product is related to health. According to the Centers for Medicare and Medicaid Services, the average American spent $5,440 for healthcare in 2002, a 36 % increase over 1994.[1] This doesn't include the cost of complementary and alternative medicine utilized by those unsatisfied with traditional medicine either. A recent survey reported out-of pocket fees paid by people for complementary and alternative medicine in the U.S. was about $47 billion. This was more than the public paid for all out-of pocket hospitalizations and about half that paid for physicians services that same year.[ii]

At the same time, improved healthcare technologies, procedures, medicines, hygiene, and sanitation have all helped to reduce mortality and morbidity rates substantially. In 1901, the average person could expect to live to the age of fifty. Today the average person can expect to live to the age of seventy-seven.[iii] Since we are living longer, it would be reasonable for us to conclude that we are healthier. But is this really the case? Statistics from the Centers For Disease Control And Prevention paints a different picture. The following table provides a report card of the nation's health:[iv]

CONDITION	% OF AMERICANS WITH CONDITION
Cardiovascular Disease	38%
Respiratory Disease	45%
Some Form of Cancer	9%
Diabetes, Ulcers, Kidney or Liver Disease	19%
Arthritis	20%
Migraines/Headaches	17%
Neck Pain	17%
Lower Back Pain	31%
Face/Jaw Pain	5%
Hearing Loss	17%
Vision Problems	10%
Loss of Teeth	17%
Some Form of Depression	39%
Nervousness/Restlessness	37%
Limitation of Physical or Social Function	43%
Overweight or Obese	65%
Cigarette Smokers	23%
Regular Alcohol Consumption	49%

These numbers are sobering and, generally speaking, they reflect a sick and suffering America. How many of these health problems have interfered with your life, or the life of someone you love? Many ailments are not even addressed in these statistics. According to the National Sleep Foundation, 62 % of Americans experience problems sleeping a few nights a week or more and 40 % of adults experience sleepiness during the day. You may say, "how does this affect health?" Drowsy driving alone accounts for 100,000 crashes in the U.S. each year.[v] Enough statistics, you get the picture. You probably wouldn't have picked up this book if you weren't concerned about your health.

To make matters worse and further complicate the situation, many people have been duped into believing the way to health is found through drugs. Pharmaceutical companies present great pictures of life and vitality during their television commercials, leading us to falsely believe taking pills will bring health. Despite their claims, drugs do not make people healthy! Drugs help in times of health crisis and have saved the lives of countless persons. But, as you will soon see, most people who develop illness live in an unhealthy state for years before the health crisis develops.

Modern medicine has brought quantity in years of life but judging by the previously mentioned statistics, where's the quality of life? Healthcare delivery in the U.S. is really set up to deliver sick care, not health care. If people were really healthy, drug companies wouldn't have so many products to sell and wouldn't be spending millions of dollars advertising their products during their two dozen daily prime-time television commercials. So now you have the facts. Let's explore what health really is and how to achieve it.

CHAPTER 2

What is Health?

Many of us are familiar with sickness. If we don't have one or more of the conditions mentioned in the last chapter, we certainly know someone who does. In our office during the weekly "Keys to Health" class we ask the question, "What does it mean to be healthy?" By far, the most common response is, "to be free of pain." Many equate the lack of symptoms with good health.

While this can be true, there are many afflictions which don't cause any symptoms until the disease process has progressed for some time. Tooth decay, heart disease, cancer, and even early stages of diabetes are just a few examples of diseases that can be underlying for years sometimes without causing any symptoms. Often the first symptom of cardiovascular disease is a heart attack or a stroke. It is not uncommon for people to have gastrointestinal ulcers and herniated spinal discs without even knowing it. These conditions are referred to by doctors as sub-clinical, where the disease state is ongoing but undetected by the patient.

If the absence of symptoms doesn't necessarily equate with health, what does it mean to be healthy? How can one describe health? A more encompassing description of health may include phrases such as:

Optimum Performance
Total Coordination of All Body Parts
Inner Balance or Homeostasis
Complete/Whole

I am rather analytical. Often when I want to find the meaning of a word or phrase I will go to my old friend Merriam-Webster. One morning a few years back I looked up the word "health" in Webster's Dictionary. Remember the "Aha Moment!" I referred to in the introduction? The first definition listed became one of those for me:

Health - The condition of being sound in body, mind, or spirit.

Immediately I said to myself, "Mind or spirit? I don't deal with the mind or spirit in my office." Could this explain why some of my patients don't respond to care and instead remain steeped in their chronic pain and illness, failed marriages, addictions, child neglect/abuse, unfulfilled lives, depressions, etc.? I began to do some soul searching. "Am I really making a difference in people's lives? Are people finding true and complete health with my care?"

Please understand it is not my intention to sing my own praises, but I feel it is important for you to have enough background to understand why this became such an "Aha Moment" for me. Since I opened my practice in 1986, I have become very successful and am blessed with the ability to heal people. Our clinic sees patients from all over the Midwest and even a few from outside the country. Almost 25 % of our patients drive more than one hour each way for care.

Usually after about one month, we repeat most of the tests performed during the initial examination to assess the progress of each patient. During this progress evaluation, we ask all our patients to rate their percentage of improvement since the beginning of their care. They report an average of almost 65 % improvement! In addition, our clinic has recently gained recognition as a training center. As a mentor, I have led several doctors into successful practice, instruct at seminars, and am a part-time faculty member of Northwestern Health Sciences University.

By all accounts, I should be satisfied with these achievements. However, with increasing frequency, I have found myself wondering how much difference I am really making in people's lives. If you are a teacher you can probably relate to some of these questions. You've heard of a mid-life crisis? Approaching my third decade in practice, I have called this my mid-practice crisis!

On that particular morning, Merriam-Webster reminded me once again there is more to health than just a healthy body. We are three-dimensional, consisting of body, mind, and spirit. Since my practice focus has been limited to the physical body, it stands to reason why some patients fall short of reaching their potential. This book was written for the purpose of speaking the *truth* about health and to address the *whole* person. I have included the definitions for the words *truth* and *whole* in the glossary at the back of this book. Please take a moment to look them up. An "Aha Moment" may be waiting for you! You may want to circle words or phrases in these definitions that represent areas of your life that could use some improvement.

A reflection of the meaning of the words whole, truth and health brings into focus a picture that many spend a lifetime trying to find. Most of us want to be whole; we search for the truth, and we desire health. Do you consider yourself to be whole? You can probably set this book down right now if you can describe yourself with words such as restored, complete, flourishing, emotionally balanced, constituting the entirety of a person's nature or development; or if you are sound in body, mind, and spirit and if you already know the truth as it relates to spiritual reality.

Although I have spent the majority of my professional life helping people achieve physical health, I have been fortunate to discover the *truth* about the mind and spirit through personal life experiences, observation, study and on occasion, just plain serendipity. On the morning of this "Aha Moment" the thought came to me that perhaps a good way to help patients find true health is by putting pen to paper. While no one but God can be all knowing and seeing,

I believe this book will provide enough truth to at least stimulate your thinking about the three dimensions of health—body, mind and spirit. I have divided our discussion into two parts. Part I will explore the five keys to physical health, and Part II will address health as it relates to the dimensions of mind and spirit.

PART I

Five Keys to Physical Health

CHAPTER 3

The "Whole" Body

The human body is amazing. Most of us don't realize just how complex it is. You have probably heard some interesting facts at one point or another and I don't wish to be redundant, but a study of the human body is not complete without appreciating just how complex it is. Over the years I have collected a few interesting facts:

- The adult heart beats about 40 million times a year and circulates 1.3 million gallons of blood every year. In one hour the heart works hard enough to produce enough energy to raise almost one ton of weight one yard from the ground.

- There is enough surface area in the lungs to cover a tennis court.

- At conception, every human spends about half an hour as a single cell.

- Our brain is more complex than the most powerful computer and has over 100 billion nerve cells.

- The central nervous system is the master control system of all functions within the body. The central nervous system is connected to every part of the body by 43 pairs of nerves. Twelve pairs to and from the brain, and 31 pairs going from the spinal cord. In all, there are about 45 miles of nerves running through our bodies.

- The human liver is our chemical factory. It can produce nearly every drug our body needs. Scientists have counted over 500 different liver functions.

- Our kidneys are the master pharmacists. The liver may produce our body's chemicals, but the kidneys determine how to use them. They decide what stays in the body and what is eliminated as waste. The kidneys maintain the internal environment essential for life.

- In one square inch of our hand we have 9 feet of blood vessels, 600 pain sensors, 9,000 nerve endings, 36 heat sensors, 75 pressure sensors, 100 sweat glands and 3 million cells.

- And one last little fact: You use an average of 43 muscles for a frown and an average of 17 muscles for a smile which proves its easier for you to smile than frown!

The individual parts of the human body are organized into systems. The major systems include: the circulatory system, respiratory system, endocrine system, musculoskeletal system, nervous system, immune system, digestive system and reproductive system. Total coordination of all of these systems is critical to optimum health. The authoritative text on human physiology used in medical and chiropractic colleges is the Textbook of Medical

Physiology, by Arthur C. Guyton, M.D. In the forward of this text Dr. Guyton writes:

> The beauty of physiology is that it attempts to integrate the individual functions of all the body's different cells and organs into a total functional whole, the human or animal body. Indeed, the life of the human being relies upon this total function, not on the functions of the single parts in isolation from the others... How are the separate organs and systems controlled in a way that no one system over-functions while others fail to provide their share? Fortunately, the body is endowed with a vast network of feedback mechanisms that account for necessary balances, without which we would not be able to live. Physiologists call this high level of internal bodily control *homeostasis.* In disease conditions, more often than not the functional balances become seriously disturbed—that is, homeostasis becomes very poor. When the disturbance is too great, the total body can no longer live."[vi]

Webster's dictionary defines homeostasis as "a relatively stable state of equilibrium or a tendency toward such a state between the different but interdependent elements or groups of elements of an organism."[vii] Understanding the principle of homeostasis is critical to grasping the delicate harmony that exists between systems of the body.

To highlight this principle let me share what became another "Aha Moment" for me during a seminar several years ago. It was February, and I suffered miserably from a cold virus. During one coughing and sneezing episode, I lamented to the doctor sitting next to me that I had been suffering with this illness for about six weeks.

Without saying a word, he grabbed a napkin, wrote something on it and then handed it over to me. Here's what he wrote:

Body Balance _____

Nutrition _____

Exercise _____

Rest _____

Positive Mental Attitude _____

He then instructed me to rate each one from one to ten (1 being bad) as to how I was doing in each area. The words he spoke next rang like a gong in my head. "Then you will have the answer as to why you are sick!" Let me repeat, "Then you will have the answer as to why you are sick!"

As I sat there completing his survey I felt like he was saying to me, "Listen dope, you are a doctor with seven years of college training. You should know that your sickness is because you haven't taken responsibility for your health in all of these key areas. You act like you are a victim of the cold virus, yet you don't exercise, you don't eat right, and you rarely get enough sleep. Is there any wonder you are sick?" In a single moment I realized that I was responsible for my own health. Don't you just hate it when you miss the obvious?

So how does this story relate to homeostasis? Health is about homeostasis. Homeostasis is about balance, and we have a large amount of control over the balance in our life. None of us will live forever, but many of us are suffering or dying needlessly because we never figure out that we have control over our homeostasis, our inner balance. Fatalities occur from car accidents every day, but statistics prove that wearing a seatbelt reduces the risk of serious injury or death. In the same way, taking responsibility for our health is like wearing a seatbelt.

A recent experience I had with a patient is a poignant reminder. This elderly woman was in declining health and suffering from cancer. She wanted to know if I could help her. As she was talking I couldn't help but notice the smell of stale cigarettes. At the top of her partially opened purse was an open pack. I knew the single most important thing she could do for her health was to quit smoking. If you smoke, I apologize for offending you, but the Surgeon General determined in 1964 that smoking kills. Here is the warning printed on every pack of cigarettes: "SURGEON GEN-ERAL'S WARNING: Smoking Causes Lung Cancer, Heart Disease, Emphysema, And May Complicate Pregnancy."

The first step towards achieving health is to understand that we are responsible for our health, not our doctor. When we are sick, our doctor is there to help us to find the proper cure, but a good doctor is also willing to help us take responsibility for our own health, just like the doctor sitting next to me at that seminar.

Alternative Medicine?

People have discovered that organized western medicine, with all its drugs and surgery, is not leading us down the path toward optimal health. In recent years we've turned to complementary and alternative medicine in droves applying the "Snoopy" approach to our health problems. One day Snoopy is shooting arrows at a fence. He shoots the arrow first and then goes to the fence and paints a bull's-eye around the arrow. Lucy asks him why he is doing this and Snoopy replies, "This way I never miss."

Often, we listen to a trusted friend or loved one who has experienced benefit with some alternative care so we try it too. A friend of mine refers to this as the "Ready–Fire–Aim" approach. When you shoot a gun without aiming you never know what you are going to hit, and someone can get hurt. Family, friends, and neighbors can offer great advice, but are they trained health care providers? Are the products they recommend appropriate for your health needs?

Several years back I recall some of my patients taking the amino acid L-Tryptophan because their friends had recommended it for sleep problems. Shortly thereafter, the FDA removed tryptophan supplements from the market because a life-threatening condition called eosinophilia-myalgia was caused by taking this supplement.

A recent survey of 31,000 adults conducted by the National Center for Complementary and Alternative Medicine showed that 36 % of U.S. adults over 18 use some form of alternative medicine. The following table lists the most often used therapies in the prior 12 months:[viii]

Natural Products	19%
Prayer by Others	24%
Deep Breathing Exercises	12%
Meditation	8%
Chiropractic	8%
Yoga	5%
Massage	5%
Diet Based Therapies	4%

Perhaps you've tried some of these alternatives. You may be asking yourself right now, "I wonder if any of these therapies can help me? I really want to take responsibility for my health but where do I begin?" Let's go back to the napkin drawing:

Body Balance _____

Nutrition _____

Exercise _____

Rest _____

Positive Mental Attitude _____

Complete this survey yourself, scoring from one to ten (one being poor and ten being excellent) the responsibility you are taking in each of these key areas of your health. Not to worry if you don't fully understand each area; simply write down what your gut tells you. For example, many people are unsure what "body balance" means. Each of these "5 Keys to Health" will be explained in more detail in upcoming chapters. You may wish to complete the survey again once you have read about each of the areas in more detail.

*At this point and certainly in the next few chapters I may be bumping up against some common preconceived ideas. Remember to keep your mind open to that which can bring you health — not blindly, but with careful consideration and sensitivity to reason and your intuition. Often when we hear something we don't necessarily like or understand we tend to write it off by rationalizing. I once heard rationalizing defined as **rational - lies**, a way of creating excuses when we hear a truth we find difficult to accept.*

CHAPTER 4

Body Balance

*"The doctor of the future will give no medicine, but will interest his patients in **the care of the human frame**, in diet, and in the cause and prevention of disease."*

T H O M A S   A .   E D I S O N

This chapter is rather long and includes a lot of technical information relating to anatomy, physiology and neurology. This is necessary to help you understand the importance of body balance to health. But if it gets to be a little too much for you, move on to the next chapter and come back to this one later. It is important that you don't get stuck here. Your health depends on it!

Is your body balanced? Do you know what it looks and feels like to have body balance; to be in alignment? If you can't answer this question with confidence you are not alone. I once asked this same question to a class of twenty-two chiropractic students and not one of them could tell me with any degree of certainty if their bodies were in balance. The simple truth is this: Most people are out of balance structurally and very few know it! I have seen thousands of patients, and I can count on two hands the number of patients I have found to be normally balanced on their first visit. Unless one experiences firsthand what it looks and feels like to be balanced structurally, it is difficult to understand how balance contributes to health and vitality. But just as maintaining the front end of your car in proper alignment improves handling and preserves the life of your tires and suspension, body balance minimizes wear and tear and improves our ride!

figure 1

Utilizing the human hand as an example, each finger represents one of the five key areas of health (Fig.1). Here the thumb represents body balance and illustrates the importance of body balance to health. The thumb is most important because the hand requires it to perform some of its most basic functions. Think of life without your thumb. In the same way, proper alignment and balance of the human frame is critical to the health and well being of an individual. An old chiropractic saying reads, "Chiropractic adds years to life and life to years!" It may just as well read, "Body balance adds years to life and life to years!"

To appreciate this critical relationship between body balance and health, four concepts must be understood:

1. There is an established normal alignment for the human body in the upright position and it can be measured.

2. Injury and stress compromise bodily alignment and balance.

3. Body imbalance affects health and well-being.

4. The body can be realigned and balanced.

Just how important is the relationship between body balance and health? I know of no other single thing that influences general health and well-being the way body balance does! (or the lack thereof) Let's take a closer look at each of these concepts.

1. There is an established normal alignment for the human body in the upright position and it can be measured.

The human eye is amazing. It has the capability of observing very minute differences. Take a look at these two identical lines. Which is closer to the top of the page?

Most people can see that the line on the right is slightly closer to the top of the page even though it is only 1/32 of an inch higher than the line on the left. The Leaning Tower of Pisa looks very crooked to the human eye, but it leans less than five degrees from vertical. In fact, it has come dangerously close to collapsing at least three times, and engineers have spent millions of dollars trying to bring it just one-half of a degree closer to vertical. Engineers and architects understand the tremendous structural stresses that occur when buildings are even slightly off center. What most people don't realize is that the same laws of physics apply to the human body.

Merriam-Webster defines alignment as "the proper positioning or state of adjustment of parts in relationship to each other." Balance is defined as "stability produced by even distribution of weight on each side of the vertical axis."[ix] These are very important words as we consider the human body. One of the first classes offered in chiropractic colleges is Medical Terminology. A section of this class includes a study of the three anatomical planes of the body (Fig. 2). Understanding these anatomical planes of the human body provides a reference for observing proper body alignment and a reference for measurement.

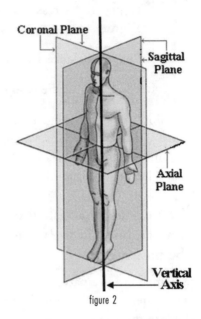

figure 2

Looking at the human body from the back, a line that divides the body into right and left sides is called the mid-sagittal line (Fig. 3). If you look at the body from the side, a line that divides the body into front and back halves is called the mid-coronal line (Fig. 4). The combination of these two lines is called the vertical axis. This line is similar to a line between the north and south poles of the earth. A spinning globe does so around its vertical axis. In the same way, the human body should be aligned to the vertical axis in the manner shown in these two pictures.

Figure 3 demonstrates normal standing posture viewed from the back or front. You will notice the vertical axis line splitting the body into two equal halves, passing through the center of the head, spine, pelvis, and exactly between the knees and ankles. In addition, lines drawn across the same reference points on each side of the head, shoulders and pelvis are all level and perpendicular to the vertical axis. Figure 4 shows normal posture from the side. The vertical axis line should pass through the centers of the ear, shoulder, hip, knee, and just in front of the ankle bone. A host of scientific evidence in the medical literature tells us that the human body should be properly balanced in this manner.

Measuring posture (and deviations from normal) is rather easy. Many scientifically proven methods for measuring posture distortion have been developed over the years. Because our eyesight is so keen, simple devices such as plumb-lines and horizontal lines on

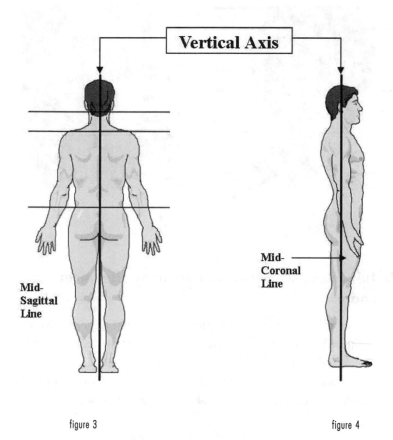

figure 3   figure 4

a wall work very well. More complex computer aided devices measure posture with even greater accuracy. Our clinic uses a variety of tools to measure body balance and postural alignment. A few of these are pictured in Figures 5 and 6. The anatometer, in particular, provides a very accurate measurement of balance and posture with scientifically proven accuracy.[x]

Horizontal Wall Lines

Anatometer II

figure 5

figure 6

2. Injury and stress compromise body alignment and balance.

Having established the normal postural alignment for the human body, the next question that must be addressed is: Can the body become misaligned sufficient to compromise balance; and if so, how? In answering this question, it is helpful to understand how the body functions to maintain normal posture and balance. We are in a gravitational field. Gravity is that constant force which is continually working to drive us into the ground.

Our body's framework consists of over 200 bones and 700 muscles. Overcoming the force of gravity while balancing on two legs requires precise control over our many bones, joints, ligaments, tendons, and muscles. The master control over all these structures is the nervous system. Think of a marionette (the puppet with strings). Your skeleton is like the puppet itself, your muscles are like the strings that attach to the different parts of the puppet, and your nervous system is the puppeteer, responsible for pulling the strings in various ways to make the puppet perform. Unlike the puppet however, the neurological control over our body is very complex. Just the simple action of standing up from a sitting position requires a myriad of separate communications between the brain and body.

The nervous system's control over the body is generally divided into two parts: sensory and motor. Sensory nerves tell the brain what is happening in the body, and motor nerves provide instructions from the brain back down to the body. Let's look at the host of neurological functions necessary to simply raise the hand. Before the brain can tell the arm where it wants it to move, it must know precisely where the arm already is. So the brain requests information from all the sensory nerves in the joints, ligaments, tendons and muscles in the arm, hand and torso. As the brain instructs the arm and hand to rise, it continually monitors the feedback from thousands of sensors in the arm and torso so it knows where the arm is in space throughout the motion.

The brain also requires continuous information from the rest of the body so that balance is maintained as the centers of gravity change during the arm movement. Balance mechanisms in the ear and brainstem as well as information from the eyes continuously monitor body position throughout the movement and help correctly identify the desired placement of the arm and hand. It is amazing to consider the infinite amount of nerve impulses that are required simply to raise the hand.

Now think of an action like a golf swing, and you can see how complex and important this two way communication between the brain and all the parts of the body really is. Police officers test this two-way communication between the brain and body in a very real way when they administer a field sobriety test. A person impaired by alcohol has difficulty even walking in a straight line. Ask that person to close their eyes or to look up while walking and the test becomes extremely difficult.

In order for the brain and nervous system to move the body into various actions and positions it must have a reference point from which to work from, a home base so to speak. This reference point is the anatomical position of neutral, which is the normal posture previously described. With great accuracy, the body has the ability to return itself to a neutral posture after every movement. This is because a normal neutral posture requires the least amount of effort for the body to maintain. Another way to describe this normal neutral posture is *Body Balance!*

So what interrupts the delicate neurological postural control over the body? One word sums it up. Injury! Trauma to the framework of the body causes joints and other tissues to be forced beyond their normal physiological limits of motion causing them to become damaged. This is much like what happens to a car door when a strong wind grabs it as it is being opened. When the door is forced beyond its mechanical limitations it no longer functions properly, and it will not return to its normal alignment with the rest of the car when it is closed. Injury to our body not only causes damage to joints, muscles, ligaments and sometimes bones, but also to delicate nerve sensors in the joints. This creates a miscommunication between the injured area and the brain. Much like a damaged car door, the body is unable to return to its normal neutral position and the result is misalignment, postural distortion and body imbalance.

Take a look at this sampling of various injuries that can cause damage to joints, ligaments, tendons and nerves sufficient to create misalignment, postural distortion and body imbalance. Do any of these ring a bell for you? Take a pen and circle any of these injuries you have had, either recently or as a child. You may be surprised at the number of opportunities you have had to become out of balance.

Obviously, there are many other ways to become injured and imbalanced. Most of us have experienced the sadness of knowing someone who has suffered physical abuse at the hand of a parent, spouse or other trusted person.

Misalignment, posture distortion and body imbalance can also occur from smaller stresses over longer periods of time. Doctors call this micro-trauma. Jobs that require prolonged sitting, bending or repetitive motions over many years induce sufficient stress to cause misalignment and postural distortion. Addiction to drugs, alcohol and cigarettes damage nerves and other tissues which control our posture as well. Considering the world in which we live, I am confident you can see why only a handful of people have walked into my office and demonstrated normal postural balance and alignment.

3. Body imbalance affects health and well-being.

To understand how body imbalance affects health, it is necessary to consider what happens to the body following trauma. The first place to look is at the weakest elements of our structural framework because these areas are usually affected first (and most) by trauma. This can be likened to the "weakest link" in a chain. A few principles apply when considering structural weaknesses in the body:

- *Smaller joints* are weaker than larger joints.
- *Smaller bones* are more fragile than larger ones.
- Joints with the *greatest motion* are weakest.
- Capsular joints are weaker than fibrous joints (discs)
- Joints with *greater weight bearing* are more susceptible to injury.

Considering these factors, one has to look no further than the spine to find the "weakest link." The spine is made up of twenty-four *small* moveable *bones* called vertebrae. There is a fibrous joint called a disc in front and two small capsular sac like joints in the rear between each vertebra of the spine. The exception to this arrangement is C-1, the top vertebra of the spine.

The common name for C-1 is Atlas (named after the mythological figure who supports the world on his shoulders). In the same way, the head, which is about the size, shape and weight of a bowling ball, is supported on the two ounce Atlas vertebra by only two small capsular joints. Interestingly, this is the only vertebra in the spine *without a fibrous disc* connecting it to the structures above and below it. This area of the spine is structurally designed to facilitate a *wide range of movement* of the head. J.V. Basmajian, MD states in *Muscles and Movements*, "The vertebral column, the great stabilizer of the trunk, also embodies mobility. However, the mobility is limited by the various ligaments, articular facets, spinous processes, intervertebral discs and other indirect factors. Although the total range of movement of the spine is wide, movement between adjacent vertebrae is quite limited, *except for the first two cervical vertebrae (the Atlas and Axis)" (emphasis added)*.[xi] The Atlas meets all the aforementioned criteria and wins the prize as the weakest joint structure in the body.

Here is a summary of this little anatomy lesson regarding trauma's effect on the body:

The spine is the most complex and weakest component of our body's framework. The upper neck (Atlas) is the weakest part of the spine. Therefore, injury and trauma will most likely cause damage in this region of the body first.

This is an "Aha Moment" that took seven years of college and a few years in practice for me to fully understand. The next logical question then becomes, "How can injury and damage to the upper neck cause postural distortion, body imbalance and detriment to health?" Let's find out.

Figure 7 demonstrates normal alignment of the neck and head. Figure 8 demonstrates the body imbalance created by a neck and head that have been misaligned due to injury. Most misalignments are not this obvious, although I have seen more than a few necks that look like this. The upper neck is not only the weakest area of the body's framework, but this region also contains the heaviest concentration of nerves, including part of the brain itself.

figure 7

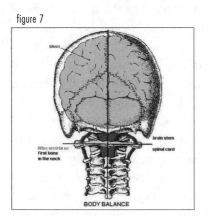

figure 8

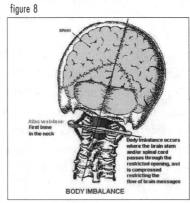

Reprinted with permission from Daniel O. Clark, D.C., www.uppercervicalillustrations.com

Most people don't realize it, but the lower end of the brainstem, called the medulla oblongata, descends into the upper neck. The top vertebra (Atlas) is a donut like bone that actually surrounds the lower brainstem. In normal alignment, the Atlas is exactly centered under an opening in the bottom of the head called the foramen magnum. Injury causes the Atlas to be shifted off center with the head, and this shifting produces neurological and postural stress. The term for this condition is the Atlas-Subluxation-Complex Syndrome. Misalignment in this region of the spine creates a host of neurological implications but only a few will be described here to prevent boredom or confusion. For a deeper look I recommend the book, *Upper Cervical Subluxation Complex*, by Dr. Kirk Eriksen (Lippincott).

The lower brainstem contains the master control centers for many functions. Some of these functions include heart rate, blood pressure, respiration, sleep regulation as well as centers for balance and posture. Much like the puppeteer, the brainstem exercises direct control over the large postural muscles that run along each side of the spine. Research has shown that a displacement of the Atlas from under the center of the skull as little as three-quarters of one degree can cause the posture muscles along the spine to pull unevenly causing the appearance of a short leg and imbalance of the entire body in the standing position (Fig. 10).[xii] In addition to the host of muscular and joint problems associated with stress on the brainstem and resulting body imbalance, people can experience symptoms as varied as high blood pressure, insomnia, and acid reflux.

The upper neck features a few other unique characteristics as well. As previously mentioned, all joints in the body contain nerve endings that sense pressure and position. They provide continuous postural information to the brain. The joints between the skull and the first two vertebrae contain more of these sensory nerves than all other joints in the body combined. In addition, the upper neck is the only place in the spine with direct neurological connections to key areas inside the brain. The implication here is that injury and damage to the upper neck most assuredly affects posture, alignment, body balance as well as other brain functions.

The hypothalamus, an area of the brain that stimulates the sympathetic nervous system, has a direct neural connection to the upper neck. Stress in the upper neck causes over-stimulation of the sympathetic nervous system which negatively affects organ function, blood flow and the immune system.[xiii] A host of clinical research supports the conclusion that many health problems are associated with damage to this region of the spine.

Figures 9 & 10 illustrate the difference in posture before and after injury. If you want to know why back pain is so prevalent, why so many people suffer from arthritis and other degenerative conditions, spend a few moments studying these two illustrations as well as

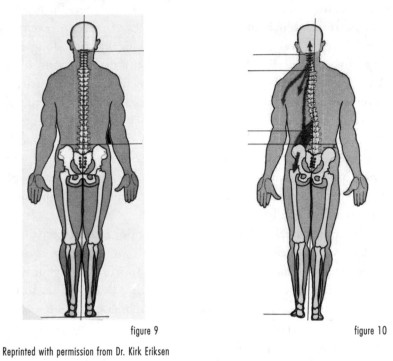

figure 9   figure 10

Reprinted with permission from Dr. Kirk Eriksen

Figures 11 & 12, which provide a close-up view of the effects of posture distortion and body imbalance. These diagrams demonstrate how posture distortion creates unequal stresses along the spine manifesting in excessive wear and tear and ultimately, joint and disc degeneration. Most disc surgeries are simply the result of years of postural imbalance and misalignment.

Anatomy of Body Imbalance

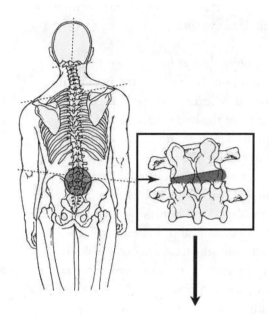

Reprinted with permission —
Eriksen, Upper Cervical
Subluxation Complex, Lippincott,
Williams & Wilkins, 2004.

figure 11

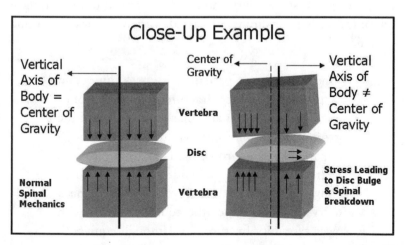

figure 12

43

Let's look at what other experts have to say about misalignment, postural distortion and body imbalance and the negative affect on health. This first study was included in an abstract written for the *American Journal of Pain Management*:

> "For many years physiologists have shown that the position of the head on the neck is vital because it governs all postural reflexes. If the head is mis-aligned, other parts of the body move in and out of line to maintain balance and thus energy is expended to counteract the effects of gravity.... Shifts in centers of gravity or postural adjustments of aging lead to intestinal diverticula, hemorrhoids, varicosities of the legs, osteoporosis, hip and foot deformities, overall poorer health, and even shortened life span.... In summary, the focal stress of spinal mis-alignment leads to muscle tension, hyperesthesia, altered circulation, and a wide variety of visceral illnesses generally associated with stress."[xiv]

Here is a summary of a research project studying the relationship between cervical spine injury and the development of fibromyalgia. Fibromyalgia is a syndrome associated with widespread pain and extreme fatigue:

> "One hundred two patients with neck injury and 59 patients with leg fractures (control group) were assessed for nonarticular tenderness and the presence of fibromyalgia syndrome.... Although no patient had a chronic pain syndrome prior to the trauma, fibromyalgia syndrome was diagnosed following injury in 21.6 % of those with neck injury versus 1.7 % of the control patients with lower extremity fractures.... Although equivocal,

some evidence has suggested that biomechanical disturbances in the cervical spine may play a role in the pathogenesis of fibromyalgia syndrome."[xv]

Here is one last research study conducted over a two month period that measured the effects of a specific upper cervical correction on eight patients presenting with high blood pressure:

"Systolic pressure was lowered by an average of 27 mmHg, and the diastolic pressure by an average of 13 mm hg. In several subjects, other symptoms such as low back pain, thoracic tightness, headaches, and general malaise, diminished following the adjustments. Those subjects who were not on medication showed the greatest change."[xvi]

Maybe you know people who really shouldn't have high blood pressure but do. Have you ever considered the possibility that a neurological problem caused by injury to the upper neck could be the cause of the high blood pressure? I could fill this book up with additional outside evidence and a second book of just my own personal experience supporting the fact that upper cervical misalignment and resulting body imbalance affects homeostasis, our inner balance, and is detrimental to health and well-being.

4. The body can be realigned and balanced.

There are many chiropractic approaches to restoring health. This section is not meant to step on any toes, but it may challenge some preconceived ideas about chiropractic. In court, when asked to provide the "whole truth," a witness has to say it like they see it. Such is the case here.

This next statement comes with a mixed blessing. Here it is, are you ready?

I have found no other means for restoring the body to proper alignment along the vertical axis besides chiropractic.

Drugs, surgery, physical therapy, acupuncture, biofeedback, nutrition; none of these can effectively restore body alignment and balance. **Chiropractic Works!** The catch is, not all chiropractic procedures accomplish adequate correction, not all chiropractors can accomplish correction and not all procedures are even chiropractic.

Mention the word chiropractic and you will get a host of reactions. There are those who love it, hate it, don't believe in it, think chiropractors are quacks, and some who are even afraid of chiropractic. The word "quack" actually came from organized medicine. In the 60's, the American Medical Association even established a committee on "Quackery" to find ways to eliminate the chiropractic profession. Much of the public fear that has surrounded the chiropractic profession was actually propagated by the medical profession! In 1987, the chiropractic profession scored a huge Supreme Court victory against the American Medical Association where it was determined that the AMA violated anti-trust laws by intentionally acting for years to destroy chiropractic, much of their tactics being misinformation to the public about chiropractic.

Even though chiropractic has helped millions of people, not all the bad press about chiropractic is unfounded. The chiropractic profession shares in that responsibility as well. I am sorry to say too many of our patients have more bad than good to say about their previous chiropractic experiences. Dr. Clarence Gonstead, a highly esteemed chiropractor noted for developing an entire system, boldly stated, **"It is not the chiropractic principle that fails but the application of the chiropractic principle that fails."** Dr. Gonstead's clinic in Wisconsin was so well known he provided an airfield and a hotel on his campus for out of town patients. I have found his statement to be true. Allow me to share with you a story about a young man that will highlight this:

> This physically fit young man, just out of high school, fell about 20 feet off a ladder and hurt his back. Upon the recommendation of his father he sought the help of a local chiropractor for the excruciating lower back pain that developed shortly after the fall. After a few visits his pain was greatly relieved. He was so impressed that he decided to go to school to become a chiropractor. But as his schooling progressed his lower back continued to become more and more of a problem. So much so that most afternoons during his second year of chiropractic college would find him laying on the floor in the back of the classroom with ice on his back to help alleviate pain. None of the many chiropractic procedures he tried were helping. He didn't even allow student doctors to examine him, only the college clinic doctors with the best reputations. He had sought care from well known chiropractors in the surrounding vicinity as well. Ultimately, all of these fine doctors would end up scratching their heads, some even suggesting the need for surgery to fuse the unstable area in his lower back.

> One day a classmate suggested this young man see a chiropractor about an hour's drive from the college, sharing how this doctor had helped a friend. In desperation, the young chiropractic student drove the forty-five minutes to Crowe Chiropractic. Dr. Crowe examined him and proceeded to take x-rays of the neck region.

Thinking this strange, the young student reminded Dr. Crowe that his problem was in the lower back, not neck.

Dr. Crowe graciously asked if anyone had helped him so far and then proceeded with the films. The student was sent home and told to come back the following day. After making the long drive the next day, Dr. Crowe laid him on his side on an odd looking table not very high off the floor. The doctor then proceeded to administer a number of little touches behind his ear. After a few minutes of this, Dr. Crowe took follow-up x-rays and sent him home with instructions to return the following week. The young student was rather dumbfounded and not very happy on his way home.

Having studied a couple of dozen chiropractic methods and experiencing even more as a patient, the young man was bewildered how this doctor could expect any results by barely touching his patients behind the ear. He felt he had wasted two days, his back still hurt, the doctor didn't address his problem, and they even charged him for care (albeit a very discounted rate) when all the previous chiropractors had extended professional courtesy. His displeasure continued until the next morning.

He had been awake for about three hours on this Saturday morning, and it was his turn to vacuum the carpet in the small mobile home he shared with his young wife. He had always dreaded this chore because it aggravated his lower back. As he was finishing the chore, it suddenly occurred to him that his lower back didn't hurt. He was so excited he yelled for his wife while reaching behind for that familiar swelling usually surrounding the painful spot. It was gone! For the first time in almost two years he had no pain in his lower back. The pain never returned. A feather-like touch under his ear had cured him!

The significance of this story is that the young student was me. Twenty-some years later, I have yet to have a recurrence of that debilitating lower back pain. What I didn't understand at the time was that Dr. Crowe had gently and precisely realigned the Atlas vertebra under my skull using a very exacting and relatively unknown procedure (more later). This firsthand experience showed me that it wasn't the chiropractic principle that had failed previously, but its application. I am very grateful to Dr. Crowe for correcting me properly and providing me with my life's work.

Does chiropractic heal everyone? Of course not; there are some conditions that don't respond to chiropractic because the illness may be caused by a loss of homeostasis that has its cause elsewhere. Sometimes the breakdown is occurring in other areas of health, and this will be addressed in subsequent chapters. More often than not however, failure to achieve proper correction is the most common reason why patients don't respond to chiropractic.

So what exactly is the chiropractic principle that Dr. Gonstead talked about and that Dr. Crowe proved trustworthy? I recently found this description on Cleveland Chiropractic College's web site. It provides a great narrative on the principle of chiropractic:

> Chiropractic health care focuses primarily on spinal function and its relationship to the nervous system and good health. The science of chiropractic is based on the premise that good health depends, in part, on a normally functioning nervous system.
>
> Chiropractic principle emphasizes that the body is a self-regulating, self-healing organism and that body function is controlled and coordinated by the

brain, spinal cord and the nerves that branch throughout the body.

The moveable bones of the spine offer protection to vulnerable communication pathways of the nervous system, specifically the spinal cord and the delicate nerve roots and spinal nerves that exit between the vertebral segments of the spinal column. A loss of normal motion or position of the spinal segments can irritate or impair nerve function, resulting in malfunction of the tissues and organs throughout the body. Doctors of chiropractic refer to this altered spinal function and its potential effect on the nervous system as the Vertebral Subluxation Complex.

The chiropractic approach to better health is to locate and remove spinal dysfunction and nerve interference, returning the body to its natural state of health and wellness.[xvii]

I wish to close this chapter by providing you with information that will help you to locate a chiropractor with the ability to restore your body's alignment and balance. There is a reason why our office has patients who will drive seven or more hours each way and pass by a hundred or more chiropractic offices to visit us. They can taste and feel what it is like to be balanced. Here are a few questions that you should ask prior to putting your health and well-being into the hands of a chiropractor:

Do the adjustments hurt?

The adage "no pain—no gain" should not apply. Spinal correction can be achieved without pain.

What criteria do you utilize to determine if a patient is in or out of proper alignment?

A good doctor should be able to explain in a concise manner objective methods for determining when a patient needs a spinal correction.

How do you know when the correction is accomplished?

Patients who are properly corrected will demonstrate improved balance and posture, less spasm and tenderness and greater mobility. A doctor should be able to explain how these post-adjustment changes are objectively measured to verify the correction.

Do you have patients who don't require correction on some of their visits?

Doctors achieving high level of spinal correction will find that patients will gradually maintain their corrections for greater length of time as care progresses. Therefore, patients should not require a correction at every visit to the office. If the chiropractor adjusts patients on every visit there is a strong possibility he/she is not correcting the spine properly or completely.

What tools do you use to measure body balance, posture distortion and nerve pressure?

Chiropractors have many diagnostic tools available to help analyze spinal subluxation and its correction. Some of these include: Observation, anatometer, leg check, palpation, thermography, surface EMG, plumb lines, computerized posture analysis, etc. I would put more confidence in a doctor who uses more than one protocol to measure body imbalance. Many doctors have these diagnostic tools but they use them for spinal screenings and initial exams, not on a visit by visit basis to assess the need for correction or verification that correction was achieved..

What protocols do you use in delivering a spinal correction to ensure you are correcting the misalignment in a mechanically sound manner?

White and Panjabi state in Clinical Biomechanics of the Spine, "The C1-C2 articulation is the most complex and difficult one to analyze." X-ray is invaluable for gaining biomechanical information about the misalignment and for determining the directional forces necessary to achieve correction. X-ray is like a window to the spine. It is nearly impossible to accurately assess all aspects of the upper neck area without using proper x-rays. Misalignments are unique to each patient and once the direction of the misalignment pattern for a patient is established, that pattern of misalignment will not usually change from visit to visit unless there is a new injury. The doctor should also be able to repeat the adjustment in the same manner each time.

How do you measure a patient's progress?

Doctors achieving high level of correction can usually demonstrate proof of the correction on follow-up x-rays. For example, if an initial side view x-ray reveals a loss of normal spinal curve (loss of curve accelerates spinal degeneration), the doctor should be able to show improvement on follow-up films taken at a later date. Nearly 100 % of our patients will demonstrate improvement of the misalignment factors on follow-up films. Other objective measurements should demonstrate improvement over time as well. Take a look at the x-rays demonstrated in Figures 13 & 14 on the next page:

What is the average length of care required for most patients?

It does not take 100 visits and two years of active care to correct a spine. Doctors who recommend care three times a week for several weeks or months are not likely to be achieving a high level of correction.

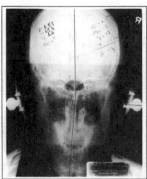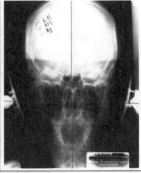

figure 13

Before and after first NUCCA hand adjustment
Submitted by Dr. Kerry Johnson

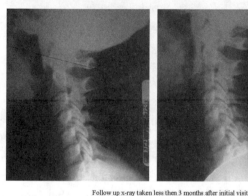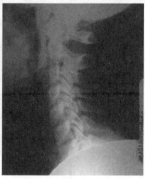

figure 14

Follow up x-ray taken less then 3 months after initial visit

Besides spinal correction, what other procedures do you utilize in your office?

Doctors who utilize many modalities of treatment are less likely to be grounded in and highly proficient in applying chiropractic procedures (or perhaps they like the extra money that comes with using additional therapies). Acupuncture, ultrasound, muscle stimulation, hot packs, stretching, massage, vibrators, traction, exercise, nutrition, biofeedback, reflexology, etc. are all valid therapeutic modalities and have a place in the chiropractor's office but none of them can take the place of a corrective adjustment.

Where did you receive your chiropractic training?

Some chiropractic colleges do a better job of training doctors in the science, art and philosophy of chiropractic than others. I chose to go to Life University because they teach sound chiropractic principles and techniques (they now teach the same procedure that helped me).

Do you have any additional post-graduate training or certification?

Doctors who take their work seriously will attend conferences, seminars and workshops relating to their chosen techniques on a regular basis. Most chiropractic organizations offer certification programs that ensure proficiency in their methods.

Did you know chiropractors utilize over 200 techniques and procedures? The drawback is that you can go to ten different chiropractors and get ten different opinions and treatments. Until the educational institutions get more serious about researching the most effective techniques and standardizing their approach to training a doctor of chiropractic, this will continue. I am not going to profess that I utilize the only sound method of delivering chiropractic correction on this planet, but I know a good approach when I see it. Chiropractors achieving high level of corrections can answer every one of the previous questions with confidence.

So which chiropractic methods are capable of delivering a spinal correction that will restore body balance? Dr. B.J Palmer, who's father D.D. Palmer discovered chiropractic, is considered to be the developer of chiropractic. By about 1930 he came to understand the relationship between the upper spine, postural alignment and body balance. People traveled to Davenport, Iowa, from all over the world for correction at the Palmer Clinic. And they didn't go there because their back hurt; they visited the Palmer Clinic because they were sick!

In the 40's and 50's, two young doctors named John Grostic and Ralph Gregory revolutionized this young science when they applied mathematical and engineering principles to the x-ray analysis, thus creating a new system of vectored light-force adjusting. Unfortunately, and for several reasons (one being they were not confident in the college's ability to teach the work), their methods failed to reach the masses of chiropractic students in accredited colleges. So for nearly forty years, the only way to learn this system was to attend their semiannual conferences. Only in recent years have methods based upon their work become a part of college curriculums around the country (I teach this work on a part-time basis at Northwestern Health Sciences University in Minneapolis). Since those early days, other sound methods for correcting the upper neck to restore body balance have been developed based upon the work of these early pioneers.

Most doctors skilled in chiropractic procedures that focus on an exacting correction of the upper neck are capable of delivering a sound spinal correction to restore body balance. Some of the methods based on the work of Palmer and Grostic include: Blair, Kale, HIO, Grostic, NUCCA, Orthospinology, S.O.N.A.R. and Atlas Orthogonal. The Academy of Upper Cervical Chiropractic Organizations has a listing of doctors who focus on the upper neck. You may be able to locate an upper cervical doctor in your area online at www.aucco.org. I utilize the procedures taught by NUCCA (an acronym for the National Upper Cervical Chiropractic Association). NUCCA has an unparalleled reputation for excellence in teaching specific upper cervical chiropractic. You can locate a NUCCA doctor on the internet at www.nucca.org.

Before we move on to the other key areas of health, I want to leave you with a few stories from patients who drive for hours, passing perhaps a hundred other chiropractic clinics, to receive care at our office:

NUCCA care at Johnson Chiropractic, P.A. was highly recommended to me by others in my area who experienced positive results. I have gone to various other doctors, medical and chiropractic, for severe migraine headaches, shoulder and back pain. In a few visits to Dr. Johnson I experienced a 50 % improvement with headaches and 75 % improvement with back and shoulder pain. I sleep better and longer. I drive about 350 miles one way for care and it is worth it. I too encourage and recommend this care to others I know.

Harriet - Roseau, MN

I was in a roll-over accident in 2002 which changed my life completely. I was unable to continue my normal duties as a husband, father, residential & light commercial contractor, and neighborly citizen after the accident. The source of my problems seemed to stem from the middle of my back and shoulder blade areas, from which would spread a knife-like pain in the mid back area to my neck, chest, arms, hands, jaws, legs, feet, along with some major digestive problems and a plugged up feeling in my nose and chest. I saw another chiropractor and physical therapist for about a year and a half. I appreciated their work but experienced only minor results. By the grace of God, I was informed about the NUCCA procedure. I immediately set an appointment with the nearest NUCCA doctor, which was Dr. Johnson, because I heard he has helped others with ailments that many are told are in your head; "see a psychologist for your situation because it may help you deal with your problem as we can find nothing wrong & can do no more for you."

Then came that most precious and phenomenal day when I received my first NUCCA spinal correction. I experienced a total relief of the knife-like pain in my mid back & within moments noticed my breathing cleared totally as well as a significant decrease in the digestive gas and burning. Until that moment I had no real hope of carrying my babies, driving with my hands on the wheel instead of propped on my lap, normal breathing, no burning & choking pain when eating, and eliminating properly. From that day forward I have continued to experience the truly life-changing benefits of NUCCA, along with my family & friends we have recommended, who have all experienced incredible results. My eight month old baby had a blocked tear duct and a goopy eye ever since birth and we wondered if NUCCA might help. The doctors at Johnson Chiropractic, P.A. didn't guarantee they could help but suggested it wouldn't hurt to have her checked. Within one week her eye completely cleared up and it has never returned! I cannot tell anyone reading enough about the benefits of this incredible science.

Jesse - Finland, MN
(Finland is a four hour drive one-way to our clinic)

I was diagnosed about fifteen years ago with fibromyalgia and have tried many different prescription medications, other chiropractors, and physical therapy to help with my symptoms. My family doctor was very supportive and sent me to a naturalistic doctor to help support me on the nutritional end and she then recommended that I see Dr. Johnson for my neck pain and to help with strengthening my immune system. Some of my complaints were fatigue, headaches, pain in my hands, legs, feet and upper back and neck.

I had an automobile accident six years ago and a biking accident two and one half years ago and they both involved neck injuries. I received chiropractic and physical therapy at the time of those accidents but I feel I did not get the correct help at that time. I did not know of the atlas and how important it was to be in alignment in that area of the spine.

I have seen Dr. Johnson for about ten weeks and have maintained my alignment for the last three weeks and am feeling well. I have no pain in my legs, feet and hands, and the pain in my upper back and neck are almost completely gone. I don't have the headaches, which before I had at least 3 times a week and were severe enough to wake me up on many nights. What a relief! I have finally found someone who can help me in controlling the symptoms of my fibromyalgia. It is great to feel I have control over something that I felt so helpless with for so many years. Mentally, this is a wonderful thing since anyone who has fought these symptoms knows how discouraging the day-to-day struggle with fatigue and pain is, especially when those around you can't see the pain you deal with daily and don't understand what you are going through.

Is has been a commitment on my part to undertake this care since I have to travel 1 hour and 45 minutes each way to get to the office from our home but it is definitely worth it!

Nancy – Nicollet, MN

Many people like Harriet, Jesse, and Nancy find themselves in our office. We have seen patients from as far away as Alaska, Hawaii, and Africa. For some, we are the last resort. And yet, there are countless others who are suffering and dying needlessly because they don't know about the vital relationship between the spine and nervous system. Don't be one of those who say, "I tried chiropractic and it didn't work." Not all chiropractic is the same and not all doctors are the same. Find a doctor who can answer the previous questions and can deliver a sound correction — a correction that will clear nervous system pressure, restore body balance and release your body's inborn ability to heal itself. Please don't wait until it is too late:

"For years, people sacrifice their health for money; then when their health is lost they sacrifice all their money trying to get it back."

UNKNOWN

Body balance adds years to life and life to years!

CHAPTER 5

Nutrition

"The doctor of the future will give no medicine, but will interest his patients in the care of the human frame, in diet, and in the cause and prevention of disease."

THOMAS A. EDISON

The coursework required to earn a Doctor of Chiropractic degree includes an extensive study in nutrition. I am just a few credits shy of earning an additional degree in nutrition. I mention this because having a knowledge base, and acting upon it, can be two different things. Honestly, nutrition has never interested me that much. The fact that I have been overweight most of my adult life is certainly evidence of this fact. Over the years, as long as I kept myself in good alignment, I could pretty much eat anything I wanted and still feel good. What I didn't realize was that my diet was causing problems that would take years to manifest.

Poor nutrition caught up with me after I turned forty. Even though I maintained good alignment, I started buying into the common notion that life after forty is downhill. That is until I rediscovered nutrition and just how important sound nutrition is to health and vitality, and how destructive poor diet is to the human body. There are truly foods that heal and foods that harm! I could write a whole separate book simply on nutrition, but other great resources are available that I will point out along the way. My goal in this chapter is to provide you with a basic overview of the major ways we sabotage our nutritional health so you can begin to understand the importance of developing strategies for setting yourself free from the foods that are harmful.

Nutrition is the relationship between food and the health of the human body. Essential nutrients required by the human body include: Carbohydrates, protein, fat, vitamins, minerals and water. As a matter of fact, these are the only substances required by the body. Our body is the most sophisticated pharmaceutical lab ever created. Using just these few essential nutrients, the body manufactures thousands of different substances (hormones, enzymes, neurotransmitters, etc.) needed by the cells of the body to maintain life and vitality. Proper nutrition supplies all of these essential nutrients in adequate balance to maintain optimum health and well-being.

figure 15

Remember the hand analogy? In this analogy, nutrition is compared to the index finger. Besides the thumb, the index finger is perhaps the most important digit for normal hand function. You can think of many functions the index finger serves. In the same way, nutrition plays a major role in a healthy life. However, opinions regarding nutrition are about as diverse as chiropractic. Bring up the subject of nutrition and everybody will have a different opinion (or a different product to sell you). Even still, most experts agree on sound fundamentals for good nutritional health, and research is proving just how important nutrition is to good health. My own experience in observing thousands of patients has taught me that simply adhering to the basics **will** eliminate most of our nutrition related health problems.

I'm sure you've heard the statement "You are what you eat!" There is some truth to this statement, but thank goodness it is not entirely accurate. If I became what I have eaten most of in my life, I would look like a pizza or an ice cream cone! We make up many excuses for the foods we eat to justify poor habits. I recall an old friend of mine who tells people he is a vegetarian. He rationalizes that because cows eat grains and grass and he eats cows, this makes him a vegetarian.

My grandparents liked food, my parents like food, and I like food. So much so that most of my family falls into the category of the 65 % of Americans who are overweight or obese. Three members of my very close family have even undergone stomach surgery to combat serious obesity. My highest weight has been 328 pounds. This would not be too bad if I were over 8 feet tall! My weight problems have not been due to a lack of knowledge. I want you to know that as we explore the whole truth about nutrition in this chapter, I am not just another doctor looking down his nose at you. I am very familiar with the personal struggles that come with poor nutrition, obesity, and the difficult challenge of developing healthier eating habits.

The Natural Approach?

People are spending millions of dollars on complementary and alternative medicine. Approximately 30 % of this spending is on some form of nutrition. Most of this expense is in the form of costly supplements. I know several chiropractors who devote nearly their entire practice to nutrition, earning a lot of money on the products they sell. Because Americans have become such "pill poppers" we look for the quick fix in our nutritional lives as well.

You probably know people who boast about "natural" pills for weight loss as well as some of these other conditions: Echinacea for colds, glucosamine sulphate for joint pain, acidophilus for stomach ailments, calcium for osteoporosis, caffeine for migraines, fish oil for rheumatoid arthritis, antioxidants for aging, tryptophan for insomnia, St. John's Wort for depression, grape seed extract for allergies, etc. The list goes on and on. There are even people who take Horny Goat Weed for sexual dysfunction! Can you see how our thinking about nutrition parallels our quick-fix, pill popping culture?

People have discovered that modern day drugs are not necessarily healthy, with all their unwanted and sometimes dangerous side effects. So as a substitute, we have turned to natural remedies in droves, rationalizing that we can get healthy without the dangerous side effects. There is some truth to this thinking, but it is much like eating meat and calling yourself a vegetarian! Anytime a chemical substance enters the body, whether derived from a plant or synthesized in a lab, it causes a pharmacological effect. In other words, it toys with the body's chemistry. So really, we are still "pill-popping" in our attempt to achieve health, we've just changed the pill.

To make matters worse, this exploration into "natural alternatives" is just that, an exploration. Often, we experiment with natural products on the recommendation of someone we know, and like the explorer, we don't know for sure what the end of the trail looks like. Many nutritional products even come to us through network marketing. A fancy presentation extolling the virtues of the product. Now we are not only taking it, but we become a distributor of the product.

Have you received an email or two advertising the latest natural wonder cure? At least organized medicine has some checks and balances through research and governmental regulation. The natural health industry is for the most part, an unregulated free-for-all. This may sound harsh, but it is the truth. We have been led to believe that natural nutritional products can only help, not harm us. Suffice it to say, it is impossible to ask some people about the side effects of using the "natural" product Ephedra for weight loss because they are no longer with us.

The body's chemistry is a very delicate balance. Scientists have counted over 500 different liver functions. Ask yourself this question: Is it wise for me to be playing chemist with the delicate balances in my body by introducing chemical substances, natural or otherwise, without a clear understanding of the short and long term effects? I recall a speech given a few years ago by a pharmacist in my hometown. He related how medical doctors were able to keep track of drugs and their interactions twenty-five years ago because there were only about 500 drugs available. Today there are thousands of drugs on the market! I remember very clearly what he said next: "Medical doctors don't have a clue what they are giving their patients today, much less how drugs interact with each other because there are too many to keep track of. Most doctors rely solely on the advice of their pharmaceutical reps in their decision making." This was a sobering statement to me, but is our natural approach to nutrition really any different?

Breakfast in Bed

When I was young I really enjoyed when my mother would let me loose in the kitchen on an occasional Saturday morning to make her and dad breakfast in bed. I usually made simple things like toast and cereal. I eventually graduated into more complex dishes like instant oatmeal or boxed pancake mixes; the ones you just add water to. One particular morning I decided to try making home-made buttermilk pancakes like my grandma used to make. I pulled my grandma's recipe from the recipe box, mixed all the ingredients in the proper order and made beautiful pancakes. I was so proud as I delivered this breakfast to mom and dad and watched them finish their plates.

I thought their faces looked a little strange as they were eating, but I didn't think anything of it until I took my first bite of the pancakes. They were horrible! How could they look so good yet taste so bad? I reviewed the recipe with my mom and together we discovered I had mixed up the amount of sugar and baking soda I was supposed to use. They rose to be nice and thick because of the extra soda I used, but the taste was ruined. I hadn't added much more baking soda than what the recipe called for, but obviously it was enough to throw off the taste of the pancakes completely. In the same way, our delicate body balances can be thrown off by seemingly little things, natural or otherwise.

Elephants

Most people have heard of the phrase, "The elephant in the middle of the room that no one is talking about." This phrase usually implies a much larger problem that is being ignored in favor of an easier way out. Our nutritional health is often like a big *elephant* in the middle of our room that no one wants to talk about. We are quick to try the latest nutritional products instead of dealing with the *elephant*. Identifying the *elephant* and getting rid of it are two separate challenges. The emphasis of this chapter is to help with the first challenge, to identify and understand the major *elephants* in our nutritional lives. I will provide some suggestions for getting rid of the *elephants*, but that challenge will be addressed in more detail later. This is because changing our nutrition requires motivation and discipline, "a change of mind" so to speak.

This next section may bump up against a few preconceived ideas. As you read, please remember overcoming inaccurate preconceived ideas creates the opportunity to experience the life-changing "Aha Moment!".

Most Americans have four large *elephants* in the middle of their room. These account for 90 % of our nutritional problems. Dealing with these four *elephants* will eliminate the need for most other nutritional interventions and their unnecessary expense. These four *elephants* are:

Portion Size

Sugar Intake

Processed Foods

Drugs/Alcohol

Elephant #1 - Portion Size

Most Americans eat much more than the body requires at each mealtime. Our waist size has directly increased to match our portion sizes. We are a society that eats out, now spending more money on eating out than on groceries. The portions we now receive (and expect) in restaurants are way more than our bodies need for sustenance. Combined with our childhood lesson to clean our plates, portion size has created a nation of overeaters.

An article in National Geographic (August 2004) provided a graphic comparison of portion sizes, past and present:

Food	Pre-1960		2004	
	Size	Calories	Size	Calories
Burger King Burger	2.8oz	202	4.3oz	310
MacDonald's Fries	2.4oz	210	7oz	610
Hershey's Candy Bar	2oz	297	7oz	1,000
Coca Cola	6.5 fl. oz	79	16oz	194
Movie Popcorn	3 cups	174	21 cups	1,700

The article cited statistics by the Centers for Disease Control and Prevention showing that the average American ate 1,775 pounds of food in 2000, up from 1,497 pounds in 1970. "Adult women are eating 335 more calories per day than they did in 1971, while adult men have upped their daily intake by 168 calories."[xviii]

The amount of food actually required by each individual varies considerably and is based on age, gender, body size and type, activity level and genetics. There are several very accurate methods for determining the amount of food required, but here I will provide you with an easy method for gaining a rough estimate of your body's requirements. Food is the body's fuel. The unit of measure for determining the energy content of food is the calorie.

Protein and Carbohydrates provide approximately 4 calories/gram and fat supplies approximately 9 calories/gram of energy. So pound for pound, fat has twice the calories as either protein or carbohydrates. To determine the amount of calories required by an individual in a day, one has to consider the Base Metabolic Rate, the amount of calories our body burns at rest and factor in the amount of activity throughout the day. Here is an easy method for determining the average daily caloric requirement:

Multiply your weight in pounds times 10 for the basal metabolic rate (BMR—calories needed if you slept all day).
  Example: 150 X 10 = 1500 calories/day
  Your weight _____ X 10 = _____ BMR calories/day

Multiply your weight times the activity factor given below.
  3 = sedentary
  5 = moderate activity
  7 = heavy activity
  10 = intense activity
  Example: 150 X 5 = 750 calories/day
  Your weight _____ X activity factor _____ = _____ activity calories

Add the result of # 1 and # 2.

Example: 1500 + 750 = 2250 calories needed each day for a moderately active person weighing 150 pounds.

Your BMR _____ + activity calories _____ = _____ total calories needed

(This is only an estimate. The actual requirement for a 150 pound person could be anywhere from 1500 (low metabolism) to as high as 3500 calories (high metabolism)).[xix]

Knowing the body's total daily calorie requirement is very useful for weight management. Regardless of what the multitude of diet schemes and programs may say, losing, gaining or maintaining weight comes down to a few simple equations:

Daily Calories Consumed = Daily Calories Required → No Change in Weight

Daily Calories Consumed > Daily Calories Required → Weight Gain

Daily Calories Consumed < Daily Calories Required → Weight Loss

The simple truth is: Eat fewer calories than what your body burns in a day, and you will lose weight. I tried to fudge with the math of these equations for years with very little success, because they simply don't add up any other way. The only way to mildly alter the equation is to change our Base Metabolic Rate (the number of calories burned at rest). Exercise, one of the keys to health we will address later in the book, is one way to mildly increase our Base Metabolic Rate.

Now let's think about what happens when we continually eat more than what our body requires. I like to use the automobile as an example. Gasoline is the fuel that provides energy to our car's engine. Every so often it is necessary to stop at a gas station and fill up the gas tank. Let's say the gas tank holds twenty gallons. What happens if we pump more than twenty gallons into the tank? Of course gas will spill out all over the ground. It will be wasted and can cause a dangerous situation. In the same way, overfilling our body with food beyond its capacity is wasteful and dangerous.

To get an idea of how this can easily occur, let's refer to the 150 pound person with a metabolism of 2250 calories/day. We'll call her Mary. Mary skips breakfast and then stops at McDonald's for lunch. She is very hungry because it's been nearly 18 hours since dinner, so she orders a "Super-Sized" Quarter Pounder with Cheese Value Meal and adds an M&M McFlurry for dessert. The calorie total for this meal is 2,220. Mary consumed her entire calorie requirement for the day in one meal! Add in a few snacks and pizza for dinner, and she will easily consume more than twice the amount of calories required to meet her body's daily calorie requirement. She spilled quite a bit of gasoline! It takes about 3500 extra calories above our daily caloric requirement to gain one pound of fat. Can you see how eating habits like this are making Americans heavier by the day? In fact, eating just 100 calories a day (one teaspoon of butter) beyond what our body burns adds up to about 10 pounds of extra weight in just one year!

There are many serious long term effects of obesity. Some of these include joint degeneration and arthritis, heart disease, high blood pressure, diabetes, indigestion, kidney disorders and certain types of cancers; not to mention the psychological and social implications. I remember the personal humiliation of being turned down for health and life insurance because I was too fat; or not being able to buckle the seat belt on an airplane and having to ask the flight attendant for an extender. Like me, I haven't met very many overweight people who were content with their situation.

Besides obesity and its effects, overeating creates other health issues as well. The Nutrition Almanac describes it this way:

Overindulgence in starchy and sweet foods may crowd out other essential foods from the diet and can therefore result in nutritional deficiency as well as obesity and tooth decay. Diets high in refined carbohydrates (sugar) are usually low in vitamins, minerals, and cellulose. Such foods as white flour (breads), white sugar, and polished rice are lacking in the B vitamins and other nutrients. Excessive consumption of these foods will perpetuate any vitamin B deficiency an individual may have. If the B vitamins are absent, carbohydrate combustion cannot take place, and indigestion, symptoms of heartburn, and nausea can result. Research continues as to whether or not such problems as diabetes, heart disease, high blood pressure, anemia, kidney disorders, and cancer can be linked to an overabundance of refined carbohydrate foods in the diet.[xx]

Excessive fat intake causes abnormally slow digestion and absorption, resulting in indigestion, and nutritional deficiency. Excess protein intake causes fluid imbalance, stress on the kidneys and leads to heart disease, constipation and osteoporosis. Think again before signing up for the popular high-protein weight loss plan! Not only is it important to consume proper amounts of carbohydrates, fat and protein, but they should be consumed in proper proportions. Once again, balance is the key. Dietary guidelines suggest the ideal diet should consist of 40 % carbohydrates, 30 % protein, and 30 % fat. When it comes to eating, balance is the key.

Having looked at some of the more chronic and long term effects of overeating, let's examine the more immediate detrimental effects of overindulgence at mealtime. Just like Mary, a person who consumes nearly their entire daily caloric requirement at one sitting creates numerous stress issues for the body. In addition to the more common symptoms of heartburn and indigestion, too much food at a sitting stresses the stomach, small intestine, pancreas, liver, adrenals, kidneys, colon, and can even trigger the body's allergic response. The added stress of overindulgence actually robs the body of essential minerals because they are used up in the process of digesting the excess amount of food. Do you struggle with low energy or depression? There is a strong connection to overeating (especially sugar), mineral depletion and loss of energy.

My grandmother used to offer this wise advice about eating:

Breakfast	-	Eat like a king
Lunch	-	Eat like a prince
Dinner	-	Eat like a pauper

If following my grandmother's advice was the single thing you decided to do after reading this chapter you will notice slow and steady improvement in your health.

Elephant #2 - Sugar Intake

The average American consumes 158 pounds of sugar annually. This is up from an average of 97 pounds in 1960. Annual sugar consumption was below 10 pounds in 1900. For the younger generations, a large portion of this increase comes in the form of soft drinks. In 1960 Americans consumed an average of 12.3 gallons of soft drinks each year. In 1999 the average was 50.8 gallons a year. Considering every 12 ounce can contains 10 teaspoons, and every gallon of soda contains .94 pounds of refined sugar, almost 48 pounds of our yearly sugar intake comes from soft drinks alone.[xxi] Remember that McFlurry from McDonald's? It has almost 14 teaspoons of sugar!

So what's so bad about having a little sweet-tooth? Some nutritionists have referred to sugar as "the worst food substance consumed by humans."[xxii] Refined sugar, in anything but very small amounts, can be very harmful to the body. It throws off many delicate body balances, greatly interfering with homeostasis. The human body must rely on its store of minerals to digest sugar. Depleting our store of minerals results in damage to the nervous system and other important body systems. People who consume large amounts of sugar not only end up becoming obese but also malnourished and addicted. Sugar consumption has been linked with diabetes, heart disease, cancer and a host of other ailments. Dr. A.B. Sabin, a prominent researcher during the polio outbreak in the 40's and 50's, in an article for the *Journal of the American Medical Association* (June 28, 1947), provided strong evidence that our society's increase in sugar consumption was at least partly responsible for the polio outbreak. Wow!

Regulation of blood sugar is a very important and delicate balance in our body. Too much (diabetes) or too little (hypoglycemia) sugar in the bloodstream is very damaging to health. When sugar is consumed, the pancreas secretes insulin which converts sugar into a substance called glycogen to counter the sudden rise of sugar pouring into the bloodstream. Then as sugar levels in the bloodstream begin to drop, the adrenal glands secret hormones which convert glycogen back into sugar to help maintain the appropriate balance of sugars in the bloodstream. Regular consumption of sugar over time causes our adrenal glands to become sluggish and blood sugar levels drop too fast after eating sugar. This creates a significant drop in energy and the brain begins to crave more. Within a half-hour the person wants to eat again. A vicious cycle is established, leading to cravings and patterns of food abuse. Another interesting fact about sugar is that it becomes addictive. It stimulates particular pleasure centers in the brain in much the same way as alcohol and nicotine.

In her book *Lick The Sugar Habit*, Nancy Appleton, PhD provides a list of 124 ways sugar can ruin your health. It lists some of sugar's metabolic consequences and is based on a variety of medical journals and scientific publications. I feel so strongly about the health consequences of sugar in our diet, I considered including the entire list here. Instead, I urge you go to her website, www.nancyappleton.com, click on "read how sugar can ruin your health" and see the list for yourself. You may be surprised by what you read. She also provides a "quiz" to help you determine if you have an addiction to sugar. Do it right now before you read any further!

I can personally relate to the harmful effects of sugar. Sugar has certainly been one of the elephants in the middle of my room! I consumed excess amounts of sugar for years and have suffered from many of the previously mentioned detrimental effects as well. Remember when I mentioned ice cream as a personal favorite? I have a particular fondness for old fashioned butter pecan ice cream. One serving (1/2 cup) contains 24 grams of sugar.[xxiii] That is equal to 6 teaspoons of sugar! Of course, my serving is a bowl full. Out of curiosity, I scooped up my typical bowl of ice cream and then measured the amount of ice cream in the bowl. I was surprised to learn that my usual serving of ice cream is about 2 1/2 cups. This three to four time a week bed-time indulgence was dumping nearly a third of a cup of refined sugar into my body each time, not to mention the 800 calories!

Many times I have consumed refined sugar and didn't even know it. Some of the yogurts with fruit can contain as much as 28 grams of sugar per serving! It pays to look at nutrition labels on foods. Ingredients are listed from the highest content to the lowest. So if you see sugar listed as one of the first four ingredients in the food, you may want to stay away from that product. Sugar is found in unlikely sources as well. Did you know that some of those delicious fast food fries are coated with sugar to make them crispy and golden brown? We'll talk about processed foods next.

A note about artificial sweeteners: Aspartame, the most common artificial sweetener, is known to be an excito-toxin, in other words it is toxic to the nervous system! I provide a short paper in my reception area about the effects of artificial sweeteners on the human body. There are a host of side effects. A few years back, my wife began noticing slurring of her speech for short periods after lunch. At lunch time she would usually consume two fountain drinks of a national brand diet cola. Her penchant for it made her resistant to read our information about artificial sweeteners, which listed slurred speech as one of the many side effects. Once she finally read the article, she chose to quit drinking diet soda and the very next afternoon she stopped having slurred speech! For more information about the dangers of artificial sweeteners go to www.sweetpoison.com.

Elephant #3 - Processed Foods

Processed foods are becoming a staple of the American diet. Most of the food at your local fast food restaurant is processed. Nearly all junk food is processed. The can of baked beans, a frozen pizza, jar of peanut butter, stick of margarine, the morning hot pocket, mayonnaise, and spaghetti sauce you buy from the grocery store? All processed! In fact, nearly all of the food in the canned, boxed, and frozen food sections of your local grocery store is processed.

Processed foods are high in calories, sugar, fat (including trans-fats), salt and low in vitamins and minerals. A few years ago I purchased nutritional software for my Palm which included a daily diet diary. I was amazed at the amount of salt, sugar and calories I was receiving from processed foods, which were the mainstay of my diet. My morning corned beef hash contained 1000mg of salt, nearly half of the sodium I should be consuming in an entire day! I visited a few websites posted by some of our favorite fast food restaurants. I also pulled four items from my own pantry and looked at their sodium content. Here is what I found:

	Calories	%of calories fromfat	Sodium
Wendy's Big Bacon Classic	580	48%	1430 mg
Whopper with Cheese	800	55%	1450 mg
Pizza Hut Super Supreme Pan (2)	680	28%	1520 mg
KFC 2-piece Breast & Thigh (OR)	740	54%	2210 mg
Bush's Best Beans (1/2 cup)			550 mg
Campbell's Chicken Gumbo Soup (1/2 cup)			970 mg
Spaghettios (1 cup)			990 mg
Prego Pasta Sauce (1/2 cup)			530 mg

According to the U.S. Department of Health, the daily intake of sodium (salt) should not exceed 2400 mg per day, or 1500 mg for those with high blood pressure. Recent evidence suggests everyone should stay below 1500 mg per day. That would completely eliminate the two-piece chicken meal at KFC. Excess salt causes high blood pressure, a major risk factor in hypertension, which is the #2 killer in the U.S. and the primary cause of strokes and heart attacks. Yet the average daily intake of salt in the American diet is estimated to be between 4,000 and 5,000 mg per day.[xxiv]

The bottom line is this: Processed foods are making America a nation of overweight, malnourished and chronically ill people. An article written by David Cameron, author of the book *Diet Liberation*, will help you to understand why:

> Have you ever seen an obese wild animal (domesti-cated animals don't count due to human influence)? I bet the answer is never. The only animals that get obese are human beings and domesticated animals

(due to human influence). And this became a common problem only after the 1950's. Why is that? We will soon see.

Out of the tens of thousands of species of animals, birds, plants, marine life, and all other life, we are the only species that have degenerative disease as a primary cause of death. We are also the only species that have obesity problems. No other creature on this planet has obesity problems.

Yet we are the only species with doctors, scientists, experts, and all that other sort of thing. At any one time, 65 % of women in the UK are on a diet. Obesity now affects almost 60 % of Americans. We have more diets, diet books, and diet foods than ever before. So why is it getting worse? If these diets worked, the problem would be reducing, not increasing. The reason lies in the nature of the foods we eat, compared to the nature of the foods pre-1950. Consider the following research.

Meso health means middle nourishment. Meso health is a condition that was discovered just before World War II by Professor Werner Kollath. He raised animals on a diet of processed foods that had been made empty of all minerals and vitamins except for thiamine, potassium sulfate, and zinc. Even though the animals were raised on a completely depleted diet, the animals grew up and initially showed no signs of disease or deficiency (by the way, we only get 10 % of our energy from food, the remaining 90 % is from air). However, when they reached adulthood they started to show degenerative signs similar to the ones you find in humans in the Western world.

The animals started developing intestinal toxemia, lost calcium from their bones and had a condition just like human osteoporosis; they started getting dental carries, started having damaged organs similar to the damage you find in humans in the Western world, and so on. When the professor gave vitamin supplements to these animals to see whether these supplements would reverse the changes, nothing happened. The only thing that was able to reverse all these changes was introduction of fresh living raw food that was composed of plenty of vegetables. This research has been confirmed many times over by scientists all over the world.

A similar experiment was done using rats. The rats were studied by a completely different set of scientists. To summarize, there were two groups of rats. One group was raised on whole wheat that was healthy and organic, and another group was raised on commercial white flour, the kind you find in the supermarket. The rats raised on white flour ended up under-sized, unable to reproduce, aggressive and hostile, and with many reports of tooth decay. The rats raised on whole wheat had no problems.

Another similar study was done using pigs. Again, one group of pigs was given a diet that was processed. And once again, they had health problems and deformed offspring. However, with pigs it only took one generation of healthy eating for the offspring to be born normal again.

As you can see, different animals eating different foods have different rates of getting sick and getting well due to the introduction of processed foods, but all of them degenerated because of cooked foods. This is the one constant: the degeneration of the body, the mind and emotions with intro- duction of a large percentage of processed and cooked foods. There is much more to this than can be said in a short article, but it begins to paint a clear picture.[xxv]

If you are over forty years old, you may remember the "Godfather of Fitness" Jack LaLanne. Jack is currently in his nineties, and he still speaks to groups all over the world about health and fitness. One of his favorite sayings is, "If man made it, don't eat it." Are you beginning to understand why? Now let's take a look at another food product that man has tinkered with.

Trans Fats

Trans fats are man-made or processed fats. Other names for trans fats include *hydrogenated vegetable oils, partially hydro- genated vegetable oil* or *trans fatty acids.* Food products like margarine and shortening are trans fats. A trans fat is made when manufacturers add hydrogen gas to vegetable oil - a process called hydrogenation. Hydrogenation turns oil into a more solid state and it increases the stability, flavor and the shelf life of food. Many manufacturers started including trans fats in their processed foods about twenty years ago. Trans fats are commonly found in the following foods:

Fast foods - Basically all fried foods
(chicken, fish, fries) and
desserts

Donuts & Muffins

Crackers

Most Cookies

Cakes, Icing, Pies

Toaster Pastries

Microwave Popcorn

Potato Chips

Candy

Salad Dressings

Many Breads

Here's what a recent feature posted on *Web*MD has to say about trans fats:

> The solidifying process - called hydrogenation - extends the shelf life of food, but it also turns polyunsaturated oils into a kind of man-made cholesterol. Trans fats can increase your level of "bad" LDL cholesterol, and may increase your risk of heart disease. What's more, trans fatty acids not only harm your health, they also block the absorption of healthy fats... Trans fats can raise your blood cholesterol as much as excess cholesterol (from the diet) can in some people.
>
> To avoid trans fats, look on the nutrition label of packaged foods. They'll appear on the ingredients list as "hydrogenated" or "partially hydrogenated" vegetable

oils. If you can, switch to products that don't use hydro-genated oils. The baked goods won't last quite as long in your pantry, but your body will benefit.[xxvi]

What is this article saying? Trans fats actually pose a higher risk of heart disease than saturated fats (animal fats), which were once considered to be the worst kind of fats. Trans fats not only raise cholesterol levels, they also deplete good cholesterol (HDL) which helps protect us from heart disease. Wow, when I was young we learned that margarine was supposed to be better for our heart than butter!

In addition to heart disease, trans fats are known to cause other serious health problems. Trans fats didn't become common in the American diet until after World War II (The very first television ad for Crisco was introduced in 1949). When ingested, trans fatty acids are converted by the body into a substance called Prostaglandin E2. Prostaglandins are hormone-like substances responsible for activation of the inflammatory response, the production of pain and fever, and an increase in free radicals, which are unstable atoms that attack healthy cells in the body. Prostaglandins also suppress immune function due to their stimulating effect on the sympathetic nervous system. What does all this mean for poor unsuspecting consumers like us? Along with heart disease, trans fats increase the likelihood of developing chronic pain disorders, allergies, premature aging, immune dysfunction and possibly even cancer. Interestingly, Prostaglandin E2 was not prevalent in the human body until after WWII.

Still not convinced you should give up those fries or chips? Consider this: The U.S. Food and Drug Administration is so concerned about this potentially serious health threat, they now require stringent nutritional labeling for products containing trans fatty acids! Okay, please allow me to toss in one last recommendation. Go rent and watch the movie *Super Size Me*. You will see a great example of how trans fats negatively affect our health.

Elephant #4 - Drugs/Alcohol

Most people are familiar with the host of harmful effects of alcohol and illicit drug use. Liver disease, brain damage, altered adrenal function, hypoglycemia and diabetes, female reproductive problems, fetal alcohol syndrome and addiction are just a few. Rather than go into a long dissertation about the physical consequences of alcohol and illicit drug use, I wish to simply repeat the old familiar phrase: Just say no! I have personally witnessed many lives devastated by what begins as a seemingly harmless fun night out.

I am also well aware of the harmful physical and emotional toll alcohol brings as well as its destructive effects on families and marriages (more later). Instead, my focus in this section is on the drugs that people consume on a regular basis and don't even think twice about. Our daily pain reliever, the morning cup of coffee, cigarettes, antibiotics and anti-depressants are just a few examples.

Caffeine

Let's begin with caffeine. Caffeine is found in common beverages such as tea and carbonated beverages, but it is the most concentrated in coffee. Caffeine is known as the world's most popular drug. Some of the short term effects of caffeine include increases in heart rate, respiration, blood pressure, stomach acid and urine production. Long term effects may include cardiac arrhythmias, heart problems, high blood pressure, headaches, poor concentration, nervousness and insomnia. Pregnant women are often advised to restrict caffeine intake because it crosses into the bloodstream of the developing fetus.

When I was about twenty-five years old I had an unforgettable firsthand experience with caffeine at a state convention of the Junior Chamber of Commerce. I had enjoyed a few alcoholic beverages the night before and was a little short of sleep. During an awards luncheon I consumed about four or five cups of coffee. Suddenly I started experiencing a strange pressure in my chest and noticed my heart beating very irregularly. I thought I was having a heart attack.

I became so worried I drove to the nearest emergency room for evaluation. The ER doctor told me I had experienced an anxiety attack secondary to the large amount of caffeine I had consumed. I switched to decaffeinated coffee, but it wasn't long before I began to have problems with decaf coffee as well. Unfortunately, the process of removing caffeine from coffee introduces several harmful chemicals into the coffee that are even more detrimental than caffeine. If you are a coffee drinker, please consider slowly cutting back to no more than one or two cups a day. A good alternative to coffee is to find a "caffeine-free" hot tea that you can develop a taste for. I actually look forward to my apple-cinnamon hot tea in the mornings now.

Remember your parents or grandparents telling you that sugar rots the teeth? If you have a sweet tooth then definitely don't add caffeine to your sugar (or sugar to your coffee). The combination of sugar and caffeine are not only highly addictive, but very harmful to our teeth. My dentist has a large poster in each of his treatment rooms showing how the acid produced by the combination of caffeine and sugar destroys tooth enamel much quicker than either acting alone. If you can't quit your soda just yet, then at least find one without caffeine.

Cigarette Smoking

Nearly everyone knows the health hazards of cigarette smoking such as cancer, lung disease, heart disease, and vascular disease. Like caffeine, nicotine is a stimulant and so it has many similar adverse effects on the body. Oxygen is the body's primary fuel source. Over time, cigarettes rob the body of needed oxygen. I have made house calls to patients bedridden with emphysema. I can't imagine a worse way to die than to be stuck in a bed for months, covered with an oxygen mask, gasping for breath while slowly being strangled.

I smoked cigarettes for ten years. When my son was about three years old, he came up to me and said, "Daddy, don't you know that smoking is bad for you?" I had to make a decision at that moment to either quit smoking or send the message to my son that it's okay to do things that are bad for you. I loved him too much to send him that message, so I took him by the hand, led him to all the places I had cigarettes stashed, and together we tossed them all in the trash. That day, seventeen years ago, was the last cigarette I smoked. Sometimes it pays to listen to our children!

Did you know the trucking industry has the highest incidence of lost work time due to lower back problems as compared with any other industry or profession in America? Why do you suppose this is? Shouldn't jobs like laying block, carpentry, roofing, and nursing put more strain on the back than sitting in a cushioned air-ride seat going down the highway? I am usually hesitant to stereotype and so I'm sorry if I offend any of our fine teamsters, but many truck drivers love their coffee and cigarettes. Caffeine, nicotine, and vibration all stimulate the part of our nervous system which causes constriction of blood vessels. Constriction of blood vessels decreases the flow of blood to the body's tissues, which leads to premature spinal disc degeneration and aging. Combine the sedentary nature of this job, prolonged sitting in a vibrating truck, the fact that tissues in the lower back are not getting adequate oxygen because coffee and cigarettes have constricted blood vessels, and it becomes easy to understand why so many truck drivers have back problems.

Over-The-Counter Pain Medications

Sales of over-the-counter pain relievers are estimated to be about $20 billion a year in the U.S. alone. The most common pain relievers are in a class of drugs called non-steroidal anti-inflammatory drugs (NSAID's). These include products such as aspirin, Tylenol, Children's Tylenol, Advil, Aleve, Nuprin, and Motrin. These drugs have been getting a lot of press in the past year alone. Recent research has exposed dangerous side effects associated with these drugs that include acute liver failure, heart attacks, and strokes! The Food and Drug Administration (FDA) is recommending stronger warnings concerning these drugs. Just in case you have missed some of the more recent reports, here's a few that should make you think twice about taking these drugs, especially on a regular basis:

- 1,055 pregnant women taking aspirin, ibuprofen (Advil, Nuprin, Motrin), naproxen (Aleve), and acetaminophen (Tylenol) had an 80% increased risk of miscarriage. (British Medical Journal)

- The pain reliever ibuprofen (Advil, Nuprin, Motrin) is associated with an increased risk of bleeding and peptic ulcers. Ibuprofen may also interfere with blood clotting and damage the kidneys. (WebMD, March 2005)

- According to a study published in the American Gastroenterological Association Journal, chronic users of non-steroidal-anti-inflammatory drugs (NSAID's) have visible damage to their small intestines. Everyday more than 30 million people take over-the-counter NSAID's (pain relievers).

- The New England Journal of Medicine (June 1999) reports that "anti-inflammatory drugs (NSAID's which include Advil, Aleve, aspirin, Motrin, Ordus and over 20 others) alone cause over 16,500 deaths and over 103,000 hospitalizations per year in the U.S. This means that NSAIDs are the 15th leading cause of death in the U.S.!

- A $26 million, five-year Alzheimer's trial was suspended by the National Institutes of Health after naproxen (Aleve) was linked to a 50 % increase in cardiovascular events (stroke, heart attacks). (US News, January 2005)

- Giving a child as little as twice the recommended dose of Children's Tylenol can damage their liver. Relatively small overdoses of acetaminophen have been blamed for liver damage and deaths in children in the U.S. (New York Times, October 19, 1997)

- According to the American Liver Foundation, acetaminophen exhibits a dose-related toxicity and toxic levels may be reached in any individual who takes more than a certain amount, particularly if alcohol is consumed. *Don't use Tylenol for a hang-over!*

If possible, *just say no* to over-the-counter medications. They are not good for you! If as little as twice the dose of Tylenol can cause acute liver failure, do you think the regular dosage is healthy for you? These drugs disrupt homeostasis, that delicate inner balance necessary for good health! Returning to the good old-fashioned hot shower, warm bath, hot water bottle, bag of ice, gentle massage, stretching exercises or a daily walk is a much safer strategy for pain relief.

Antibiotics

Antibiotics have been the "Cinderella-story" of health care since their discovery in the 1940's. Many lives have been saved by antibiotics, even though improved sanitation, hygiene, and nutrition are the key factors largely responsible for the containment of disease in this country. Antibiotics are so popular that consumers are often reluctant to leave their doctor's office without a prescription. This is in light of the fact that antibiotics will not work for viruses such as colds, flu, coughs, bronchitis, runny noses, sore throats (except Strep), and most ear infections. More recent information about the overuse of antibiotics in the US is creating great concern in the medical community. Here's what the Centers for Disease Control has posted on their website (www.cdc.gov/getsmart) about antibiotics:

> Today, virtually all important bacterial infections in the United States and throughout the world are becoming resistant. For this reason, antibiotic resistance is among CDC's top concerns. Antibiotic resistance can cause significant danger and suffering for children and adults who have common infections, once easily treatable with antibiotics. **Antibiotic resistance has been called one of the world's most pressing public health problems** (emphasis added).

Another serious health consequence of taking antibiotic drugs is not as well understood by an uninformed public (or even some doctors) but poses a risk that rivals antibiotic resistance. Have you ever experienced digestive problems while taking antibiotics? Antibiotics upset the normal balance in our digestive tract, known as the intestinal flora. The intestinal flora contains beneficial bacteria that protect our intestinal lining and help to break down foods into digestible particles.

Since antibiotics are not able to distinguish between beneficial and harmful bacteria, they destroy the good bacteria in our intestine, which can lead to indigestion and several other health problems. Acidophilus and lactobacillus are two examples of good bacteria that are destroyed by antibiotic drugs. In the absence of these beneficial intestinal bacteria, an overgrowth of antibiotic resistant bacteria, parasites, yeasts and toxicity usually develops. A particular type of yeast, Candida, converts into a fungal or *mycelial* form when the normal bacterial environment is upset and can be very damaging to health.

Some of the more common digestive complaints such as heartburn, reflux disease, flatulence, constipation, and diarrhea occur in the absence of healthy intestinal flora. Many other "stress related" conditions such as weight gain, anxiety, joint pain and swelling, headaches, skin conditions, food cravings, insomnia, loss of energy and forgetfulness can be attributed to antibiotic drug therapy. Wow! It looks like Cinderella is turning into the ugly step-sister!

You may want to consider reading the book *Lifeforce* by Dr. Jeffrey McCombs if you are experiencing one or more of the above mentioned symptoms or if antibiotics have been a part of your medicine cabinet. I found his detoxification plan to be very helpful in eliminating many of these symptoms that have bothered me. The "Lifeforce Plan" also helped me to change some eating habits necessary for weight loss. More information about this detoxification program is available on-line at www.lifeforceplan.com.

What About Some of Our Other Favorite Drugs?

Antidepressants have also been in the news lately. New studies are showing that widely prescribed antidepressants may actually trigger suicidal behavior. A recent FDA analysis showed that children taking antidepressants had twice the rate of suicidal thoughts. Prozac is currently the only FDA-approved drug to treat pediatric depression, but physicians are also prescribing others like Paxil and Zoloft. The number of children (as young as two to four years old) taking psychiatric, behavior changing drugs is increasing exponentially. Here's what Dr. Ian Smith, a TIME medical contributor, has to say about this alarming trend:

First, it's extremely troubling that young kids are being prescribed drugs that have serious side effects and that have never been studied in that age group. These toddlers on drugs could foretell a future peopled entirely by lifelong, glazed-over Prozac users who have no built-in abilities to deal with stress or sadness.[xxvii]

While we're on the subject of children, let's talk about Ritalin. Ten million prescriptions of Ritalin are filled each year for children with Attention Deficit Hyperactive Disorder (ADHD). The most commonly reported side effects of Ritalin, an amphetamine like drug, include loss of appetite, weight loss, insomnia, depression, headaches, stomach aches, irritability, bed-wetting and dizziness. More severe psychological problems have been reported as well. Children can become depressed, lethargic, robot-like and withdrawn on stimulants such as Ritalin. Withdrawal from Ritalin can cause emotional suffering that includes depression, exhaustion, and suicide. For this reason, concerns exist regarding its potential for causing long term drug dependence. Scientific evidence has demonstrated that Ritalin actually has properties similar to cocaine! WebMD (March 2005) reported that **every** child included in a study on Ritalin experienced chromosome abnormalities three months after starting the drug. Chromosome damage is linked to a heightened cancer risk and other health problems.

Prudence Required!

Please understand that I am not advocating the avoidance of all drugs. There are serious health problems that require drugs. A Type-II diabetic must have insulin to survive. A patient of mine was told by her medical doctor that she would have died from a recent bout of pneumonia had she not been given a course of antibiotics.

There is a place for drugs in health care, but my emphasis here is to help you understand the consequences of over-reliance on drugs, especially our over-the-counter favorites. The Physicians Desk reference, commonly referred to as the drug bible, shows us that few, if any, drugs are healthy for us. Drugs always come with unhealthy side effects. Again, we have to take responsibility for our health, including the types and amounts of medicines we take.

Eating Elephants

After reading this chapter you may be saying to yourself, "I'm doing a lot of things right; just a couple of little changes needed." However, if you're like me and so many others, you may be wondering where in the world to begin. You're thinking, "How can I possibly move these elephants out of my room?" There is no quick fix when it comes to righting our nutritional wrongs and no easy way out. This is a job for the crock pot, not the microwave! You may have heard the question: "How do you eat an elephant?" The answer is: **"One Bite at a Time!"** Begin by doing an honest assessment of your nutritional health. Score yourself from 1 to 10 (10 meaning you don't have any problems in that area) for each of the following nutritional problem areas:

Portion Size _____

Sugar _____

Processed Foods _____

Drugs/Alcohol _____

Sometimes the first step in healing is to recognize the problem. Unfortunately, knowing the truth about nutrition doesn't always lead to success in changing our lifestyle and eating habits. If a much less intelligent animal eats and drinks only those things that are good for it, why do we humans have so much difficulty consuming only those foods and drinks that will properly nourish our bodies? A famous Christian writer once stated, "I don't understand myself at all, for I really want to do what is right, but I don't do it. Instead, I do the very thing I hate."[xxviii] As you continue reading I am confident you will better understand the complexity of our design and in doing so, you will learn how you can begin to make choices that will lead you to health.

At the end of this book I will share with you step-by-step how I got rid of the elephants, regained the health and vitality I had been robbed of for years, and how I lost 100 pounds in the process (see pictures on next page). However, without reading the rest of the book it may not make much sense to you, so don't just skip to the end!

My friends and I in 1993

My family and I in 2005

CHAPTER 6
Exercise

figure 16

In our ongoing analogy, the middle finger represents exercise, the third key to physical health. Like the index finger, the middle finger is a very important digit to overall hand function, and it is often the strongest of the four fingers. In the same way our middle finger lends strength to the hand, exercise provides our body with the strength it needs to overcome our gravitational environment here on earth. Many great books and videos are available to help you select and perform a proper exercise program so in this chapter I will stick to a more broad discussion of exercise and its importance to health.

The old adage, "If you don't use it, you lose it!" certainly applies to the human body. The human body is designed for movement, exertion, and physical labor. Maybe you or someone you know has had knee surgery. It used to be that doctors would immobilize the knee for four to six weeks following surgery. They would then prescribe an aggressive physical therapy regimen to restore strength and flexibility. Very seldom would a patient ever achieve normal range of motion or strength in the knee following the surgery. Today, immediately after knee surgery the leg is placed into a CPM (continuous passive motion) device to keep the knee moving. A more complete healing and normal range of motion is achieved even with patients who have had total reconstruction. This same principle applies to exercise in general. The more we use our bodies, the more our bodies will do for us.

America is not only getting heavier, but we are becoming more sedentary. Automation in industry and computer technology has made the workplace easier and less physical. Yard chores have been made easier with riding lawn mowers, blowers, and vacuums. Inventions like television, computers, the X-Box and the internet have brought our kids in from their more physical outdoor activities. Let's not forget about elevators and escalators. Perhaps the worst robber of exercise is the automobile. Some statistics show the average American walks as little as 400 yards a day. As a whole, we are much less active than even twenty years ago, and we are paying the price.

Walking

Our body responds to the physical stress of walking in very beneficial ways. Weight bearing exercise stresses our skeletal frame so that calcium is deposited into our bones in proportion to the stress placed on them. A leg bone that is fractured and placed in a cast will lose about 30 % of its bone mass in just six weeks. A major concern in the weightless environment of space is the loss of bone density that astronauts encounter. There is nothing better than a good walking program to prevent osteoporosis. Walking is beneficial for us in many other ways as well.

A recent Harvard Medical School study shows that walking at a moderate pace (3 mph) for up to 3 hours a week—or 30 minutes a day—can cut the risk of heart disease in women by as much as 40 %. This is the same benefit you would get from aerobics, jogging, or other vigorous exercise. The benefits to men are comparable.[xxix] Along with its benefits to the heart, walking:

- improves circulation
- helps breathing
- combats depression
- bolsters the immune system
- helps prevent certain cancers
- helps prevent osteoporosis
- helps prevent and control diabetes

Flexibility

Flexible muscles are very necessary to prevent joint and nerve injury. I can't tell you how many times patients have come into our office with an extremely painful lower back and when I ask them how it happened they tell me, "I just bent over!" Upon examination I usually find very tight hamstring muscles (the muscles on the back side of the upper leg). When the hamstrings are too tight, the smaller joints and discs in the lower back have to work overtime and are exposed to injury because the pelvis and much stronger hip joints don't flex forward as far as they should during the course of bending.

Just as flexible muscles are important to the athlete for preventing injuries, good flexibility often minimizes the damage from our inevitable slips and falls. Have you ever slipped on steps and reached for the railing? During this event, the arm will be stretched out above the head by as much as 160 - 180 degrees. Someone with a normal upward arm motion of 135 - 145 degrees is much less likely to sustain serious injury to their shoulder as opposed to someone with only 90 degrees of normal movement. This is the reason that flexibility is so crucial to the longevity of professional athletes.

There is another reason why it is so important for joints to be able to function in their entire range of motion. Loss of movement in a joint has the potential for triggering pain, which is actually a reflex signal to the brain that the joint is not functioning properly. Many incidences of chronic pain can be greatly reduced by improving flexibility. There have been remarkable advances in techniques for improving flexibility that are easy to learn and require very little time. Take some time to search out the flexibility training program that is right for you. You can find good flexibility training programs at health clubs, community education programs, your doctor's office and on-line. Always check with your doctor before beginning any exercise program to determine if it is the right one for you.

Joint movement that accompanies exercise also stimulates lubrication of the joint and prevents osteoarthritis. A great amount of misunderstanding exists regarding arthritis. Many people blame hard work during their lifetime as major contributor to their arthritis. Movement of joints within their physiological limits actually promotes healthy cartilage and the production of lubricating fluid in the joints. As mentioned previously, arthritis is primarily caused by abnormal motion and unequal distribution of weight across joints due to misalignment, not from using the joints. The spinal misalignment caused by a fall from the hay loft as a young boy is much more likely to cause arthritis for a farmer than lifting hay bales and milking cows.

Cardiovascular Exercise

The benefit of cardiovascular exercise has long since been proven. Cardiovascular exercise is basically exercise for the heart, lungs, and blood vessels in the body. Oxygen contained in the air we breathe is the major fuel source for the body. The heart, lungs, and circulatory system deliver this fuel to all parts of the body. It is essential that this system be in good working order. The better the heart, lungs, and circulatory system can provide oxygen to all parts of the body, the healthier the body is. Cardiovascular exercise not only improves the function of the entire body, but it improves the health of the heart, lungs, and blood vessels themselves. Cardiovascular exercise involves maintaining a heart rate at a sustained target level for at least twenty minutes, a minimum of at least three times a week. The following formula is used to determine target heart rate:

220 Minus Your Age = Maximum Heart Rate
80 % of Maximum Heart Rate = Target Heart Rate For
Cardiovascular Workout

Example: A forty-two year old has a Maximum Heart Rate of 178 (220 - 42 = 178). 80 % of 178 is 142. This individual should maintain a heart rate of around 142 beats per minute during the course of exercise for at least twenty minutes, a minimum of three times per week.

Feeling for the pulse of the carotid artery in the neck (just left or right of the Adam's Apple) is the easiest way to check your pulse during exercise. Count the number of beats you feel in 6 seconds and multiply that number by 10 to determine your heart rate. Many exercise apparatuses at health clubs will automatically check your pulse to help you monitor your heart rate during exercise. Inexpensive wristwatch devices are also available to help you monitor heart rate during exercise.

Cardiovascular exercise also stimulates the body's production of endorphins which are hormones that act as natural pain relievers. We feel good when we exercise. Long distance runners and cyclists go crazy if they can't exercise because they miss the "runner's high" that accompanies the production of these hormones. You don't have to be a long distance runner to benefit from this natural feel-good hormone production. Even mild regular exercise will produce endorphins sufficient to make you feel good.

Weight Loss

Exercise burns calories, stimulates body functions and increases metabolism. This is very helpful when trying to lose weight. Here are a few examples of the calories burned by a few common exercises:

Exercise	Duration	Calories Burned
Brisk Walk	45 Minutes	462
Stationary Bike	30 Minutes	493
Lap Swimming	40 Minutes	575
Jog/Walk	45 Minutes	554
Golf/Carry Clubs	2 Hours	1108

Not only do we receive the benefit of the calories burned during the exercise, but our metabolism is raised for up to five hours after the exercise, using up even more calories. Regular exercise is much more effective than a cup of coffee or a Mountain Dew when it comes to providing needed energy. I have a little saying in my office: "In order to get energy, you have to give energy!" If you are lacking in energy, regular exercise will help you get it back. Regular exercise is wonderful for the libido as well!

Pump it Up!

Resistance training is very helpful in gaining and maintaining sufficient muscle mass to protect and support the body properly. Not only should muscles be flexible, but they should have sufficient strength. Resistance training is a fancy way of saying weight lifting. The principle here is that stressing a muscle strengthens it. The ability of an individual to successfully move around in our gravitational environment is directly proportional to the strength of the individual. Health clubs have very nice apparatuses arranged in circuits to provide strength training for all the body's major muscle groups. The key to success in resistance training at a health club is to start slow and make sure you are properly trained to use the equipment. Working out with a certified trainer for your first few sessions is a wise choice. For those who don't have access to a health club or gym, there are numerous resistance exercises that can be done without any equipment. Examples include the good old-fashioned push-ups and sit-ups. Again, many videos are available to show you how to do resistance exercise without going to the gym. Pilates exercise is one such program.

Allow me to add one last word about exercise. Most people don't exercise because they don't like to! Even when they make up their mind to exercise, they often give up on it before they have had a chance to get into a more enjoyable habit. When starting an exercise program, find something you enjoy doing. If you hate water, don't swim for exercise. Rather, if you love to play basketball, join a league where you can play every week.

Variety is the spice of life, especially when it comes to exercise. Find fun and different things to do to get your exercise in. If you're married, make a commitment with your spouse to turn the TV off after dinner and go for a walk, a bicycle ride or to the gym. If you can find an exercise that you and your spouse like to do together you will have an immediate accountability partner. A few years ago, my wife and I discovered that we love to cross-country ski together. For the first time since I can remember we actually look forward to Minnesota winters. Trying to find time for exercise can be a challenge. Once when I was complaining about not having enough time to exercise I was reminded by a friend that "scheduling my priorities is better than prioritizing my schedule." If you make exercise a priority in your life you will schedule it.

When it comes to exercise, I am reminded of two sayings that have stuck with me over the years. When our children were little we used to read and sing to them at bedtime. One of their favorite songs was a silly song called the *Tortoise and the Hare.* The song ended with the line, "Slow and steady wins the race!" Similarly, a few years ago one of the pastors at our church entitled his message, "It's Not How You Start, It's How You Finish!" Can you see how these sayings apply to exercise?

It is wise to have an evaluation by a qualified health professional before beginning any exercise program. Your individual health status may require an exercise regimen tailor made to suit your individual situation. Also, if you haven't exercised for years don't start by walking five miles or biking twenty-five miles. You will set yourself up for injury and then will have to quit exercising so you can heal from the injury caused by the exercise.

CHAPTER 7

Rest

"What is without periods of rest will not endure."
"Take rest; a field that is rested gives a beautiful crop."

OVID

figure 17

We're coming into the home stretch in our discussion of the five keys to physical health. Rest is represented here by the ring finger. Just as a beautiful ring adds brilliance to our appearance, a rested body provides a beauty that is often noticed by others. We are simply nicer and more attractive to others when we are well rested.

Today, time is almost more of a commodity than money. Advances in technology were supposed to save us time, but the opposite has occurred. We've had to increase our standard of living to pay for all the time saving technology and conveniences. Today's automobiles have more powerful computers than the ones used to put a man on the moon! But an average full size SUV costs nearly $40,000! In the market where I live, a middle of the road house can cost $400,000. After that comes designer clothes, food, the monthly cell phone, cable, and internet bills, not to mention the new computer every two years, and of course that high definition big screen TV. Once all this is paid for we then have to figure out how to pay for our kids' $20,000+ per year college bills and their $25,000 weddings.

America is indeed a rich country, but our higher standard of living usually requires two or more household incomes and longer work hours. Factor in time for recreation, family, school activities, church, housework, meals, exercise, television, internet, etc. and something has to give. Our life becomes a case of robbing Peter to pay Paul, and sleep is definitely Peter! Can you honestly say that you get enough sleep? The human body requires sleep. It is like plugging into a battery charger for the night. Our heart, nervous system, joints and muscles as well as many other body systems need their daily rest or they will not function properly. Let's cover a few specifics.

The Spine and Nervous System

Our spine has twenty-three sac like structures that position between every vertebra called intervertebral discs. Discs contain large amounts of a watery fluid. Did you know that the average adult male is almost an inch taller in the morning than in the evening? If you are tall like me, you have to adjust the rear view mirror in your car in the morning and evening to account for the change in height throughout the day.

During the day gravity works on the upright spine to slowly force fluid out of the discs. Since almost one-fourth of the height of our spine is from our discs, the slow decrease in disc height from this fluid loss creates a measurable difference in overall height from morning to evening. During a night's rest in a horizontal position, the pressure outside of the discs becomes greater than within, and fluid is slowly replaced inside the discs. This process is called osmosis, and it is the only source of nutrition for spinal discs because they have no direct blood supply after age eighteen. Discs are very important structures to the overall health of the spine because they provide separation between each vertebra, allowing room for pairs of nerves to exit between each vertebra. As discs become flattened, nerves get pinched and irritated. If our brain cannot properly communicate with all parts of our body due to disc narrowing, health is adversely affected. Discs require seven to eight hours of horizontal rest to fully refill. A contributing factor to spinal disc degeneration is not getting enough rest at night.

Sleep is very important for the brain as well. Science has proven that brain activity slows greatly after sustained periods of wakefulness. This accounts for our loss of concentration, memory, and function when we are sleep deprived. Sufficient sleep is needed for our nervous system to work properly. Parts of the brain actually perform many of their functions during sleep. Release of growth hormone in children and young adults takes place during sleep. Most cells of the body show an increase in production and less breakdown during deep sleep. Some of the effects of sleep deprivation on the brain include: impairment of memory and physical performance, reduced ability to carry out mathematical calculations, suppressed immune function, mood swings and even hallucinations. Animal studies have shown that sleep deprivation can greatly affect our health. Here is a summary of one such study:

> The normal life span of rats is two to three years. However, rats deprived of sleep live for only about three weeks. They also develop abnormally low body temperatures and sores on their tails and paws. The sores probably develop because of impairment of the rats' immune systems.[xxx]

The brain goes through four stages of sleep followed by a type of sleep called REM. Without going into detail, each stage of sleep is characterized by a different brain wave. This means that the brain is performing different functions as it proceeds through the different stages of sleep. Robbing the brain of any of these stages is like using a virus infected computer before the anti-virus program has had a chance to run through all of its operations necessary to repair the computer.

"Tick-Tock"

When we sleep is nearly as important as the length of time we sleep. Our bodies have their own built in clocks, much like a washing machine that goes through its different cycles as it washes clothes. We have a built in twenty-four hour clock. Our bodies go through biological variations every twenty-four hours. These variations are controlled by our body's biological clock and are called circadian rhythms. Circadian rhythms are influenced greatly by light. Light sets our biological clock. That is why our bodies are best suited for wakefulness during the day and sleep at night. Very few adults who wake up at the same time every morning require an alarm clock. This can be a bit frustrating during the weekend when we are trying to claim that extra hour or two of sleep. When we toy with our normal sleep schedule, it can have serious consequences to our health and well-being.

When I was in college I took a "graveyard" shift cleaning the floors of a large supermarket. I started at 11 PM and finished at about 7 AM. I would rush home and grab about two hours of sleep before my 10 AM class. Then at about 3 PM I would sleep for another two or three hours. Occasionally I would sleep from 8:00 - 10:30 PM, when I wasn't hanging out with my future wife. I lasted about two months before I ended up in the hospital with an unidentified virus! The body's clock is so precise it knows when the body should be resting. I have talked with many patients working swing shifts or nighttime shifts who tell me they never get used to sleeping during the day.

Our bodies have built in mechanisms for letting us know when we need more sleep. I could often trace my children's illnesses to the previous week when they were "burning the candle at both ends." As we age, our bodies don't respond so acutely because we build up a tolerance to sleep deprivation. But if you're one of the 39 % of Americans who struggle with depression, take a look at your schedule and make sleep a priority. If you have chronic illness, make sleep a priority. Don't be like the rats!

If Only I Could Sleep!

For many people it's not their busy schedules or work hours that are keeping them from getting enough rest. They just can't sleep. They either can't fall asleep, or they sleep for a few hours and then toss and turn the rest of the night. This can be devastating, especially with the many demands placed on us today. Here are some effective ways to improve your sleep:

- Make sure you have a good bed. Like Goldilocks, it has to be just right, not too hard or too soft. Go to the furniture store with a book and lay down on a bed for a half-hour (it is best to go during non-busy hours). If you have to roll over in that time, it may not be the bed for you. Spend money on a good bed. Many cheaper beds are comfortable at first, but two years later they are starting to lose their support capabilities. Also, don't keep a bed for more than ten years. Beds wear out! I am often amazed when I ask patients if they have a good bed. They'll say, "Sure doc, I have a great bed!" Then when I ask them how old it is I hear, "It's only eighteen years old!" We spend a third of our life in bed. Don't be cheap when it becomes time to buy a bed.

- Use a good pillow. A down/feather pillow works well for those who don't have allergies to them. Their flexibility allows for a good fit for different sizes of people and body types. The drawback to these is they will not hold their shape throughout the night to provide a constant support for the head and neck. A lot of chiropractors sell cervical support pillows. I have tried many different types of pillows and got tired of their one size fits all approach. Also, many of them are designed for back sleepers and not side sleepers. A few years ago I came across the Therapeutica Pillow. It has worked well for hundreds of my patients. It is engineered for back and side sleeping and comes in five different sizes. The company guarantees satisfaction and provides an unmatched warranty. Go to www.therapeutica.com to find a distributor near you. Make sure a qualified health professional fits you for the proper size.

- Establish a consistent bedtime and wake-up time. Go with your body's clock, don't try to fight it. It takes discipline to stick to a consistent sleep schedule, but your body will like you for following it. Even that extra hour or two on the weekend can throw off the body's clock. Many of my patients who suffer with migraine headaches have shared with me that sleeping in on the weekend will trigger a migraine.

- Establish a bedtime routine that will relax you and prepare you for sleep. A bubble bath, a good book, calming music, prayer, quiet time on the deck, or a cup of caffeine-free tea are just some ideas to relax and prepare you for bed.

- Don't go to bed worried or angry. The Bible offers some good advice about worry and anger. First, about worry: "Can all your worries add a single moment to your life? Of course not."[xxxi] Second, about anger: "Don't let the sun go down while you are angry, for anger gives a mighty foothold to the Devil."[xxxii] This advice is sometimes easier said than done. It can be very difficult to change how we feel. We may be very justified in our anger or worry. It takes practice to learn to let go of our anger, especially when it is justified or the person sleeping next to us is the cause of our anger. If possible, work out your differences before going to bed. Better to lose an hour of sleep than an entire night. When I am worried about something I try to follow this wise advice: I count my blessings instead of sheep!

- Avoid eating large meals after 6 PM and avoid large quantities of protein during the evening meal. Our bodies receive the optimum amount of energy from protein about seven-eight hours after it is ingested. So a large steak or pizza at 7 PM may find you wide awake at 2 AM with energy to burn!

- As with exercise, schedule your priorities rather than prioritizing your schedule. Realize that you are not Superman or Wonder Woman. Our bodies are designed to accomplish only so much. Maybe it's time to give up something for the sake of a little peace, sanity, and rest in your life.

- If you are having trouble sleeping during the night then don't take naps during the day unless you absolutely have to.

- Make time for regular exercise, but avoid exercising at least three hours before going to bed. Our bodies require this time to cool down and restore physiological functions to a resting level.

- Don't expose yourself to bright light before going to bed. It can mess with your biological clock and circadian rhythms.

- If you have been in bed for at least thirty minutes without being able to fall asleep, don't stay there and toss and turn. Get out of bed and go through your bedtime ritual again (i.e., reading, hot bath).

- Find a chiropractor who can properly align your upper neck. I have often told my staff that if I were going to market my practice as a specialty practice it would be in the area of sleep disorders. A vast majority of our patients are amazed by how much better they sleep after their balance has been restored. The centers of the brain that secrete serotonin, the hormone that controls sleep, are located in the lower end of the brainstem adjacent to the top vertebra in the neck, and are greatly affected by the Atlas Subluxation Complex Syndrome (see Chapter 4).

In closing this chapter, I am reminded of my grandma's favorite TV program, *The Lawrence Welk Show.* I remember as a child sitting on her living room floor on Saturday evenings watching this musical variety show with her and the family. After all these years I can still remember the closing song, and I wish to share a portion of it with you: "Good night – sleep tight – and pleasant dreams to you!"

CHAPTER 8

Positive Mental Attitude

"Attitude is a little thing that makes a big difference."

WINSTON CHURCHILL

figure 18

The last key to health is our attitude and it is represented in our analogy by the little finger. We don't often give a lot of attention to mental attitude, but it can control our health and well-being in much the same way a little girl has her daddy wrapped around her little finger! I will be addressing the role of the mind in greater detail later, but in this chapter I simply want to provide you with a brief overview of our attitudes and how they affect health and healing.

The human mind is an amazing creation. No computer can ever match its complexity. Here are some interesting facts about the brain:

- When you are born, your brain weighs about a pound. But by age six, it weighs three pounds. What happens? Learning to stand, talk, and walk creates a web of connections in your head—two pounds worth!

- Your brain weight accounts for about 2 % of your body weight. But your brain uses 20 % of your body's oxygen supply and 20 to 30 % of your body's energy.

- Your brain has about 100 billion neurons. A typical brain cell has from 1,000 to 10,000 connections to other brain cells.

- The right side of your brain controls the left side of your body, and the left side of your brain controls the right side of your body.

- Your brain is full of nerve cells, but it has no pain receptors. Doctors can operate on your brain while you're awake—and you won't feel a thing!

- A message for action travels from your brain to your muscles as fast as 250 miles per hour.[xxxiii]

With all that is known about the brain, scientists haven't even scratched the surface in their investigation into the brain and its relationship to attitude, emotion, free will, and the relationship to health. Neuroscientists can't really even tell us where exactly in the brain the function of emotion takes place. Scientists do agree however, that attitudes and emotions are extremely important for survival, adaptation, and overall health.

The Placebo Effect

An interesting phenomenon often occurs in healthcare. A Canadian doctor I know describes it like this: "There have been over 5,000 different approaches to improving health through the ages that have proven to be effective and almost all of them have a common theme. If the doctor believes what he/she is doing works, and the patient believes the doctor, then the healing response of the body will be triggered." I believe his statement has merit. The confidence I display and loving care I provide in my office directly affects the outcome of a great many of my patients. There is a saying in healthcare that I always try to remember, "Patients don't care how much you know until they know how much you care." Why is this statement so true? Because of the role our mind plays in healing.

On the flip-side, I sometimes wonder why certain patients ever come into my office. They are the "Doubting Thomas" types. These patients are usually referred by someone they trust, but they have made up their mind from the get-go that I am probably not going to help them. And guess what? I often don't. The made-up mind can be a powerful force, for good or bad, when it comes to healing. The body is inherently designed to be a self healing organism. But sometimes the difference between sickness and health is located between the ears.

Mind Games

Our attitude about ourselves is greatly influenced by the fact that we are all born and raised in an imperfect world, by imperfect parents and teachers, hanging out with imperfect peers and exposed to many injustices. Emotional and mental baggage carried from our childhood influences our entire being. This baggage can manifest itself in unresolved resentment and forgiveness issues which can lead to anger, bitterness, and a life filled with pessimism. Often we don't even realize it's there.

Anger, bitterness, and a poor self-image lead to sickness and poor health. I've heard more than one holistically trained doctor connect cancer, especially in women, as stemming from the influence of longstanding issues relating to un-forgiveness. I'm not suggesting that everyone with cancer should look for someone to forgive, but I agree that the underlying stress of harboring resentment towards others negatively affects our health.

Some people don't feel they deserve to be healthy and so they do things to sabotage their health without even realizing it. Eating disorders, smoking, alcohol and drug abuse, are usually only outward manifestations of inner turmoil. Our attitude about our self often affects every aspect of our physical health and well-being. I can relate to this type of sabotage because I have lived it. I battled addictions for many years. If reading this short chapter has struck a cord with you, I am here to tell you there is hope. There is a way to overcome self defeating and harmful attitudes and get on the path that brings life, health, happiness, and peace. In fact, it's why I wrote this book. So keep reading!

I want to end this chapter with a short narrative on the importance of attitude:

Attitude

By Chuck Swindoll

The longer I live, the more I realize the impact of attitude on life.
Attitude to me is more important than facts.
It's more important than the past, than education, than money,
than circumstances, than failures, than successes,
than what other people think or do.
It's more important than appearance, giftedness, or skill.

It will make or break a company, a church, a home.
The remarkable thing is we have a choice every day
regarding the attitude we will embrace for that day.
We cannot change the inevitable.
The only thing we can do is play on the one string we have,
and that is our attitude.
I am convinced that life is 10 % what happens to me,
and 90 % how I react to it.
And so it is with you.

PART II

The Master Key to Health and Wholeness – A Sound Mind and Spirit

CHAPTER 9

Mind and Spirit
Which Worldview?

Do you remember Webster's definition of health? It is the condition of being sound in body, mind, and spirit. If this is indeed an accurate definition, and the goal is to achieve true health, then any comprehensive study of health must include mind and spirit. Examination of the mind and spirit is often avoided in healthcare because so many different and sometimes conflicting worldviews exist. A worldview is like a pair of glasses through which we view the world. Everybody has a unique prescription. If you're still reading at this point in the book, I'm confident you have deemed trustworthy most of what has been written so far.

Even though taking responsibility for your physical health may be a daunting task, we're most likely wearing similar glasses up to this point because scientific evidence supporting its benefit is difficult to challenge. It is rather easy to use the tools of science in our study of the human body because the human body is readily visible, especially with today's technology. Discovering the truth about our mind and spirit presents a particular challenge to science because of their metaphysical nature. In other words, because the function of mind and spirit are not readily observed and measurable, there are particular limitations when we attempt to use science as the primary tool for discovery.

In order to support reasonable conclusions regarding the mind and spirit, it is necessary to include other disciplines such as philosophy and theology. It is at this point where people tend to put on different glasses, so to speak. It is interesting to note however, that the gap between these fields of study and science is rapidly closing. For example, scientific advances in our understanding of the vast universe as well as the tiny atom are leading us closer to the conclusion that an intelligent design was at work from the beginning of time. In other words, science is beginning to reveal just how unlikely it is that our existence occurred from mere random chance.

Research conducted by the pollster George Barna has suggested that nearly 80 % of Americans believe in God, and over 60 % believe in God as described in the Bible. If this research is accurate, then 60 - 80 % of you should not have difficulty accepting the truth presented in the following chapters. This is because the pair of glasses we will use to examine mind and spirit is based on a Christian worldview. For the other 20 - 40 %, I don't expect you to blindly accept my words. The remainder of this chapter will make the case for why I believe the Christian worldview represents the pair of glasses that will provide us with the clearest vision of mind and spirit. Feel free to use your own reason, judgment, and experience to test and approve the truthfulness of what comes next.

If you haven't already guessed it, you have come to the place in this book where your preconceived ideas about God (atheistic, agnostic, cultic, or otherwise) can prevent you from having an "Aha Moment!" Read on with an open mind. If you do, I am confident you will find the truth about mind and spirit. Also, when I make a reference to "man" in the upcoming chapters I am utilizing the non-gender sense of the word for the purpose of consistency because other sources I will be quoting use the term in this sense.

Accepting the truthfulness about the mind and spirit based upon a Christian worldview requires the settling of two very important issues:

1. Evolution vs. intelligent design. Do we exist because of random chance and natural selection (Darwin's theory) or as a result of a creator, a supernatural intelligence (God)?

2. If we exist as a result of intelligent design then what does God look like? Of all the religious doctrines describing God, does Jesus Christ really represent the one true God?

Sufficient evidence exists to support the conclusion that we exist as a result of intelligent design and that God is represented in the person of Jesus Christ as described in the Bible. There are many resources available on this subject but I have selected two books, *The Case for a Creator* and *The Case for Christ* (Zondervan). Both of these books were written by Lee Strobel, an atheistic journalist who investigated the scientific evidence for intelligent design and for Jesus Christ. I chose these books because they are well written, supported by scientific fact, and they are relatively easy to read should you desire further investigation.

God vs. Darwin

An examination of the book *The Case for a Creator* provides an exhaustive list of evidence supporting Intelligent Design. Below is a summary of several key points made in the book along with the page numbers for easy reference:

The Problem with Evolution and Natural Selection

• Biological machines (such as an individual living cell) require all of their individual parts to function. Such a complex system cannot be built by a Darwinian process of natural selection because natural selection only helps complex organisms to survive to the next generation, the survival of the fittest. A simple mousetrap provides us with a good illustration of this point. A mousetrap consists of a flat wooden platform, a metal hammer, a spring to press against the platform and the hammer when the trap is charged, then finally, a metal bar that connects to the catch and holds the hammer back when the trap is charged. Take away any of these parts and the mousetrap is broken. It simply doesn't work at all. In the same way, "evolution can't produce an irreducibly complex biological machine (such as a living cell) suddenly, all at once, because it's much too complicated. The odds against that would be prohibitive. And you can't produce it directly by numerous, successive, slight modifications of a precursor system, because any precursor system would be missing a part and consequently couldn't function (like the mousetrap). There would be no reason for it to exist. And natural selection chooses systems that are already working." (pages 79, 198)

- Regarding the famous Miller Experiment (where this scientist created amino acids—the building blocks of life—in an atmosphere he likened to primitive earth): "Put a sterile, balanced solution in a test tube. Then put in a single living cell and poke a hole in it so that its contents leak into the solution. Now the test tube has all the molecules you would need to create a living cell, right? You would already have accomplished far more than what the Miller experiment ever could— you've got all the components you need for life.... The problem is you can't make a living cell. There's not even any point in trying. It would be like a physicist doing an experiment to see if he can get a rock to fall upwards all the way to the moon. The problem of assembling the right parts in the right way at the right time and at the right place, while keeping out the wrong material, is simply insurmountable. Explaining the origin of life naturalistically is just silly." (page 39)

- Francis Crick, who shared the Nobel Prize for discovering the molecular structure of DNA, says it like this: "An honest man, armed with all the knowledge available to us now, could only state that in some sense, the origin of life appears at the moment to be almost a miracle, so many are the conditions which would have had to have been satisfied to get it going." (page 42)

- Darwin believed that future fossil discoveries would help fill the self-admitted huge gaps in his evolutionary tree of life. The fossil record that has advanced more than a century since Darwin's evolutionary tree of life has actually done just the opposite. "There are no fossils that support Darwin's theory of a long history of divergence." In other words, the fossil record shows no evidence of a slow transition from jellyfish, sponges and worms to insects, crabs and vertebrates. (pages 43-44)

Evidence from the Cosmos and Physics

- Scientific study in the past fifty years has led most experts to agree that the universe had a beginning. Previous predictions about the Big Bang have since been consistently verified by scientific data.

"Obviously if there was a beginning, *something* had to bring the universe into existence.... Given that whatever begins to exist has a cause and that the universe began to exist, there *must* be some sort of transcendent cause for the origin of the universe." (pages 106, 108)

• The universe is incredibly fine tuned to support life on earth. If gravitational, electromagnetic, and nuclear forces or any other fundamental properties of the universe were altered even slightly, life would be impossible. "In light of the infinitesimal odds of getting all the right dial settings for the constants of physics, the forces of nature, and other physical laws and principles necessary for life, it seems fruitless to try to explain away all of this fine tuning as merely the product of happenstance.... If I bet you a thousand dollars that I could flip a coin and get heads fifty times in a row, and then proceed to do it, you wouldn't accept that. You'd know that the odds against that are so improbable—about one chance in a million billion—that it's extraordinarily unlikely to happen. The fact that I was able to do it against such monumental odds would be strong evidence to you that the game was rigged. That is designed.... The extraordinary fine-tuning of the laws and constants of nature, their beauty, their discoverability, their intelligibility—all of this combines to make the God hypothesis the most reasonable choice we have. All other theories fall short." (pages 135, 136, 149)

Evidence from Chemistry and Biology

• Consider what is needed to form a simple protein molecule by chance. "First, you need the right bonds between the amino acids. Second, amino acids come in right-handed and left-handed versions, and you've got to get only left-handed ones. Third, the amino acids must link up in a specified sequence, like letters in a sentence. Run the odds of these things falling into place on their own, and you find that the probabilities of forming a rather short functional protein at random would be one chance in a hundred thousand trillion trillion trillion trillion trillion trillion trillion trillion trillion trillion. That's a ten with 125 zeros after it! And that would only be one protein molecule—a minimally complex cell would need between three hundred and five hundred protein molecules." (page 229)

• Naturalistic means cannot come close to explaining how the amazing amount of biological information got into the six feet of DNA coiled inside every one of our body's one hundred trillion cells. "We know books and computer codes are designed by intelligence, and the presence of this type of information in DNA also implies an intelligent source." (page 282)

• Complex microscopic contraptions such as cilia and flagella or the intricate process of blood clotting cannot be explained by numerous, successive, slight modifications, the hallmark of Darwinian theory. (pages 201-211)

I have only scratched the surface regarding the evidence for intelligent design (God). Other topics presented in the book that provide evidence supporting the existence of God include:

• Our solar system's position in the Milky Way Galaxy.

• The earth's position in our own solar system.

- Chemistry and physics cannot explain consciousness. Introspection, sensations, thoughts, emotions, desires, beliefs, and free choices are functions of our consciousness. "Darwinian philosopher Michael Ruse candidly conceded that 'no one, certainly not the Darwinian as such, seems to have any answer' to the consciousness issue. Nobel Prize-winning neurophysiologist John C. Eccles concluded from the evidence 'that there is what we might call a supernatural origin of my unique self-conscious mind or my unique selfhood or soul.'" (page 283)

Examining the evidence should lead one to conclude that it takes more faith to believe that we evolved from a single cell amoeba than to believe that an intelligent creator (God) exists and is responsible for the incredible life sustaining universe in which we live.

The Apostle Paul, in his New Testament letter to the Romans, summarizes this subject very well. Do you see any similarities with the previous arguments for intelligent design?

"For since the creation of the world God's
invisible qualities—his eternal power and
divine nature—have been clearly seen,
being understood from what has been made,
so that men are without excuse."

R O M A N S   1 : 2 0

Having made the case for the existence of God, now let's examine the exact nature of God. The doctrine of Jesus Christ as the Messiah, the Anointed One of God, is utterly dependent upon the truthfulness of the biblical account of Jesus' existence, his death on a cross, and his resurrection from the dead. No other leader of a major religion has demonstrated the ability to overcome death. So let's take a close look at the claims of Christianity as they relate to the deity of Jesus Christ.

Is Jesus Really God?

An examination of the book *The Case for Christ* provides an exhaustive list of evidence supporting the claim made in the Bible that Jesus is in fact the Son of God, the Messiah that had been foretold about in the Old Testament scriptures. Below is a summary of several key points made in Lee Strobel's book along with the page numbers for easy reference:

Evidence from the Multiple Biographies of Jesus

- There are four separate people who wrote biographies concerning the life and existence of Jesus. These biographies are contained in the four gospel accounts written by Matthew, Mark, Luke and John.

- Even liberal scholars have dated the gospel accounts of Jesus to have been written within thirty-sixty years following the crucifixion of Jesus. The significance of this is that they were written within the lifetime of various eyewitnesses of the life of Jesus, "including hostile witnesses who would have served as a corrective if false teachings about Jesus were going around." (page 33)

- "The two earliest biographies of Alexander the Great were written by Arrian and Plutarch more than four hundred years after Alexander's death in 323 B.C., yet historians consider them to be generally trustworthy." (page 33)

- Even though the biographies about Jesus contained in the gospels were written thirty-sixty years after the death of Jesus, evidence contained in the book of Acts and the writings of the Apostle Paul demonstrate that key facts about "Jesus' death for our sins, plus a detailed list of those to whom he appeared in resurrected form—all dating back to within two to five years of the events themselves! That's not later mythology from forty or more years down the road.... Christian belief in the Resurrection, though not yet written down, can be dated to within two years of that very event.... Now you're not comparing thirty to sixty years with the five hundred years that's generally acceptable for other data—you're talking about two!" (page 35)

- There are various inconsistencies among the various gospel accounts. "If the gospels were too consistent, that in itself would invalidate them as independent witnesses.... This would have raised charges that the authors had conspired among themselves to coordinate their stories in advance.... There is enough of a discrepancy to show that there could have been no previous concert among them; and at the same time such substantial agreement as to show that they all were independent narrators of the same great transaction." (pages 45, 46)

Corroborating Evidence - Other Written Accounts

- Other written accounts of Jesus outside of the Bible have been proven to exist. A Jewish Pharisee named Joshephus wrote about Jesus in 93 A.D. A Roman historian named Taciturn wrote about Jesus in A.D. 115. A man named Thallus wrote a history of the eastern Mediterranean in A.D. 52. It made reference to the darkness that the gospels had written about as Jesus hung on the cross. (pages 78, 82, 84)

Archeological Evidence

• No archeological discovery has disproved a biblical reference. "Further, archeology has established that Luke, who wrote about one-quarter of the New Testament, was an especially careful historian. Concluded one expert, 'If Luke was so painstakingly accurate in his historical reporting (of minor details), on what logical basis may we assume he was credulous or inaccurate in his reporting of matters that were far more important, not only to him but to others as well?' Like, for instance, the resurrection of Jesus." (page 260)

Analyzing Jesus Himself

• "The evidence for concluding that Jesus intended to stand in the very place of God is absolutely convincing." In other words, Jesus actually believed he was the Son of God, the Anointed One of God, the Messiah. (page 142)

• Given that Jesus intended to claim to be the Son of God then one has to explore the possibility that he was crazy. "Well-known psychologist Gary Collins said Jesus exhibited no inappropriate emotions, was in contact with reality, was brilliant and had amazing insights into human nature, and enjoyed deep and abiding relationships. 'I just don't see signs that Jesus was suffering from any known mental illness.'" (page 261)

Does Jesus Fit the Profile of the Messiah that was Foretold?

• "Hundreds of years before Jesus was born, prophets foretold (in writing) the coming of the Messiah, or the Anointed One, who would redeem God's people. In effect, dozens of these Old Testament prophecies created a fingerprint that only the true Messiah could fit." There are at least forty-eight Old Testament prophecies that were fulfilled by Jesus. The probability of fulfilling all these messianic prophecies is one chance in a trillion trillion trillion trillion trillion trillion trillion trillion trillion trillion trillion trillion trillion trillion. (Where have we seen this number before?) (pages 183, 262)

Eyewitness Accounts

• In his New Testament letter to the Corinthians, Paul states that Jesus appeared to over 500 people after his resurrection from the dead. This is the earliest and best authenticated account. Paul also stated that most of them were still living. "He would never have included this phrase if he wasn't absolutely confident that these people would confirm that they really did see Jesus alive." (pages 231, 232)

The Disciples' 180° Change in Behavior After the Resurrection

• Evidence for the resurrection of Jesus from the dead is exhibited in the behavior of his disciples. "When Jesus was crucified, his followers were discouraged and depressed. They no longer had confidence that Jesus had been sent by God, because they believed anyone crucified was accursed by God. They also had been taught that God would not let his Messiah suffer death. So they dispersed. The Jesus movement was all but stopped in its tracks. Then after a short period of time, we see them abandoning their occupations, regathering, and committing themselves to spreading a very specific message—that Jesus Christ was the Messiah of God who died on a cross, returned to life, and was seen alive by them. They were willing to spend the rest of their lives proclaiming this, without any payoff from a human point of view…. They often went without food, slept exposed to the elements, were ridiculed, beaten, imprisoned. And finally, most of them were executed in torturous ways. For what? For good intentions? No, because they were convinced beyond a shadow of a doubt that they had seen Jesus Christ alive from the dead…. When you've got eleven credible people with no ulterior motives, with nothing to gain and a lot to lose, who all agree they observed something with their own eyes—now you've got some difficulty explaining that away." (pages 246, 247)

• Saul of Tarsus was a Jewish Pharisee. He took it upon himself to execute Christians when he had the chance. Then suddenly he not only stops persecuting Christians, but he actually joins them! Paul, as he later became known, has written two-thirds of the New Testament including a reminder to the Corinthians that he performed miracles when he was with them there. He would have been foolish to suggest this had they knew it wasn't true. What changed this man? "It's not the simple fact that Paul changed his views. You have to explain how he had this particular change of belief that completely went against his upbringing; how he saw the risen Christ in a public event that was witnessed by others, even though they didn't understand it; and how he performed miracles to back up his claim to being an apostle." (pages 248, 249)

The Sudden Change in Jewish Tradition

• Jesus changed key social structures in the Jewish tradition that had been passed on for countless generations without change. "Now a rabbi named Jesus appears from a lower-class region. He teaches for three years, gathers a following of lower- and middle-class people, gets in trouble with the authorities, and gets crucified along with thirty thousand other Jewish men who are executed during this time period. But five weeks after he is crucified, over ten thousand Jews are following him and claiming that he is the initiator of a new religion." Suddenly, no more animal sacrifices, Moses' law no longer brought salvation, no more Saturday obser-vance of the Sabbath, God is no longer monotheistic but consists of Father, Son and Holy Spirit, and finally, their picture of the Messiah suddenly changed from the political leader they had been waiting for to someone who suffered and died for the forgiveness of sins. (page 250, 251).

Explosion of a New Religion

• We're almost home! "Let's think about the start of the Christian church. There's no question it began shortly after the death of Jesus and spread so rapidly that within a period of maybe twenty years it had even reached Caesar's palace in Rome. Not only that, but this movement triumphed over a number of competing ideologies and eventually overwhelmed the entire Roman empire. Now, if you were a martian looking down on the first century, would you think Christianity or the Roman Empire would survive? You probably wouldn't put money on a ragtag group of people whose primary message was that a crucified carpenter from an obscure village had triumphed over the grave. Yet it was so successful that today we name our children Peter and Paul and our dogs Caesar and Nero!" (page 254)

Please allow me one last quote from Lee's book. "Sir Lionel Luckhoo was a brilliant and savvy attorney whose astounding 245 consecutive murder acquittals earned him a place in *The Guinness World Book of Records* as the world's most successful lawyer. Knighted twice by Queen Elizabeth, this former justice and diplomat subjected the historical facts about the Resurrection to his own rigorous analysis for several years before declaring, 'I say unequivocally that the evidence for the resurrection of Jesus Christ is so overwhelming that it compels acceptance by proof which leaves absolutely no room for doubt.'"

So, for the 60 % of you who believe that Jesus Christ is who he claimed to be, I trust I was "preaching to the choir" and that your faith has been bolstered by these excerpts. But perhaps you've yet to settle this issue in your mind. That's okay! It is my hope that you are at least willing to appreciate and consider the supporting facts about the Christian worldview I brought to the table and that you are compelled in some way to read on. But here's one last question to ponder: What happened two thousand years ago that was so significant that the world's calendar became based upon the life of one man named Jesus?

Mind and Spirit - Put Your Glasses On!

In 1994 I participated in a course on Christian living and the following Bible verse was the focus of one particular week's study:

> *"For the word of God is living and active.*
> *Sharper than any double-edged sword,*
> *it penetrates even to dividing soul and spirit,*
> *joints and marrow; it judges the thoughts*
> *and attitudes of the heart."*
>
> HEBREWS 4:12

My analytical nature led me to ask the instructor this question, "What is the difference between soul and spirit?" I appreciated his honest response when he said, "That is a good question! Why don't you try to find the answer and report back to the class." I decided to take him seriously because I had wondered what the soul was as far back as my simple childhood bedtime prayers, "I pray the Lord my *soul* to take."

I began a six month investigation on the difference between soul and spirit, researching many books and interviewing several pastors. Most of the pastors provided me with rather vague answers, giving me the impression they didn't have a good understanding of the difference themselves.

The clearest explanation of the difference between soul and spirit came one day about four months into my study from what I considered to be a very unlikely source, a man named Jim Sky. Jim is a Native American from northern Wisconsin, who had spent nearly ten years in prison for drug trafficking and had lived on the streets of downtown St. Paul for several years as a homeless drunk. In the middle of his despair, he was led to the Lord and has since become a pastor. To my amazement, he explained the difference between soul and spirit very simply, concisely, and in a way that made perfect sense to me. He also recommended a book on the subject entitled *The Spiritual Man* by Watchman Nee.

I hunted down the book and began reading. The reading was very intense and the writing style difficult to follow at times. I found my best reading time to be in the morning when I was completely fresh and alert. By the time I finished the fourth chapter I had a newfound understanding of how the human being is made and how we are designed to function in our environment on this earth. A couple of months later, I summarized what I had learned regarding the difference between soul and spirit for the class. Just like me, they were amazed at how the puzzle pieces fit together so well, and they were very grateful for my explanation. My purpose here is to provide you with the same anatomy lesson in a way that will help you understand the complex design of the human being. I believe this will lead you to a much greater self awareness of the source of your attitudes, behaviors, and motivations. Self-awareness is often the first step to productive and positive change.

You may be asking yourself, "What do *soul and spirit* have to do with *mind and spirit*, the subject of this chapter?" The answer is simple. Pastor Sky and Watchman Nee helped me to understand that our mind is simply a part of our soul. The human being is really three dimensional, consisting of body, soul, and spirit. So when I talk about the soul, please know that the mind is just one element of the soul. Following is a description of the characteristics of the three dimensional nature of the human being, body, soul, and spirit. You may wish to spend a few minutes reflecting on these three dimensions:

Body	Soul	Spirit
Physical Being	Mind	Conscience
Relates To Material World	Will	Intuition
through Senses	Emotions	Communion
(World-Conscious)	(Self-Conscious)	(God-Conscious)

Don't be concerned if you don't completely understand this breakdown of body, soul and spirit. You have most likely heard the terms conscience, intuition, communion, mind, will, and emotions. But if you're like most people, you've probably not seen these words described under the context of soul and spirit until now, or you may not even understand their meanings. Neither had I until my little research project in 1994. Once I describe in more detail the workings of body, soul and spirit and how they interact, I am confident you will understand, as I have, what it means to be "whole."

CHAPTER 10

Body, Soul, and Spirit
The Perfect Design

I always looked at human beings as being comprised of body and soul, the outer visible part and the more nebulous spiritual inner part. But the Bible makes a distinction between the soul and spirit of the individual. First Thessalonians 5:23 reads, "May your whole spirit, soul and body be kept blameless at the coming of our Lord Jesus Christ." Here the scriptures identify us as being three dimensional, consisting of body, soul, and spirit. The verse mentioned previously out of the book of Hebrews also separates the soul and spirit.

The Bible distinguishes between God's Spirit and our spirit as well. Romans 8:16 reads, "The Spirit himself testifies with our spirit that we are God's children." There are several other scripture references to man's spirit as being separate from the Spirit of God. A few passages include Zechariah 12:1, First Corinthians 2:11, Psalm 34:18 and Matthew 26:41.

A look at the original language used to write the Bible can often provide a more complete understanding of the meaning behind scripture passages. The account of God creating Adam in Genesis

2:7 is one such example: "the Lord God formed the man from the dust of the ground (body) and breathed into his nostrils the breath of life (spirit), and the man became a living being (soul)." The words I added in parentheses are the English translation of the original Hebrew text. Watchman Nee, in his book *The Spiritual Man*, describes this particular passage in this way: "'Formed man of dust from the ground' refers to man's body; 'breathed into his nostrils the breath of life' refers to man's spirit as it came from God; and 'man became a living soul' refers to man's soul when the body was quickened by the spirit and brought into being a living and self-conscious man."[xxxiv]

Our soul expresses our individuality. It is what makes the human being different from any other creature on the planet. It is the part of us in which the body and spirit are merged. It is in the soul that we find the individual's free will. I am going to quote Watchman Nee one more time because he provides a very good analogy to describe the soul. Like me, you may have to read it a couple of times to really grasp its meaning:

> God treated man's soul as something unique. As the angels were created as spirits, so man was created predominantly as a living soul. Man not only had a body, a body with the breath of life; he became a living soul as well. Thus we find later in the scriptures that God often referred to men as "souls." Why? Because what the man is depends on how his soul is. His soul represents him and expresses his individuality. It is the organ of man's free will, the organ in which spirit and body are completely merged. If man's soul wills to obey God, it will allow the spirit to rule over the man as ordered by God. The soul, if it chooses, also can suppress the spirit and take some other delight as lord of the man. This trinity of spirit, soul and

body may be partially illustrated by a light bulb. Within the bulb, which can represent the total man, there are electricity, light and wire. The spirit is like the electricity, the soul the light, and body the wire. Electricity is the cause of the light while light is the effect of electricity. Wire is the material substance for carrying the electricity as well as for manifesting the light. The combination of spirit and body produces soul, that which is unique to man. As electricity, carried by the wire, is expressed in light, so spirit acts upon the soul and the soul, in turn, expresses itself through the body... It is through the corporal body that man comes into contact with the material world. Hence we may label the body as that part which gives us *world-consciousness*. The soul comprises the intellect which aids us in the present state of existence and the emotions which proceed from the senses. Since the soul belongs to man's own self and reveals his personality, it is termed the part of *self-consciousness*. The spirit is that part by which we commune with God and by which alone we are able to apprehend and worship Him. Because it tells us of our relationship with God, the spirit is called the element of *God-consciousness*. God dwells in the spirit, self dwells in the soul, while senses dwell in the body.[xxxv]

A further explanation of each of our three dimensions may help you to more fully understand how we are made.

The Spirit

Again, the only way we can comprehend and commune with God is through our spirit.

If this is true, then it becomes essential for us to know that we have a spirit and how it functions. The Bible, combined with few millennia of study, teach us that man's spirit is comprised of conscience, intuition, and communion. The **conscience** is the discerning part of the spirit. It makes spontaneous judgments as to right and wrong, independent of any learned knowledge. In fact, our educated mind will often reason or rationalize (remember *rational-lies?*) what our conscience has judged as right or wrong. My wife used to refer to this as the "little man" inside of her warning her when she was about to do something she shouldn't. **Intuition** is our spiritual antenna, so to speak. It is that part of our spirit that receives direct revelation from God's Spirit. Intuition is knowledge that comes to us without any help from the mind, will, or emotion. Our mind simply helps us to interpret that which our intuition has already received from God. It is different from a "mother's intuition" in that it does not come from our educated mind. It is commonly known as "that still small voice" from God. **Communion** is that part of our spirit that worships God. Our soul cannot comprehend God, nor does God relate directly with our soul. It is only through the spirit that God can be comprehended and worshipped.

Soul

The soul is who we are; it is what makes us unique in God's creation and from each other. The soul expresses our individual personality. You may recall from history that a sailing ship's manifest (the list of people aboard) would list the number of "souls" aboard. Our personality is made up of the sum of our mind, will, and emotions. Thinking, reasoning, choice, decisions, love, values are but a few elements of the soul. The **mind** is that part of our soul which is responsible for thought, reasoning, and knowledge. Intelligence and wisdom as well as foolishness arise in the mind. All learning, except for the direct comprehension of God, takes place in the mind. The **will**, or volition, is that part of our soul that gives us the ability to choose. The mind can help us to examine options, but it is our will that is the ultimate decision-maker. We choose "To" or "Not To." Without free will we would be nothing more than robots. Our individual tastes, our likes and dislikes, are found in our **emotions**. Feelings such as love, hate, joy, anger, fear, resentment and peace are expressed in our emotions. It can be said then that our soul is comprised of our *thinker*, our *chooser* and our *feeler*. In his book, Watchman Nee lists pages of scripture references which support this teaching about soul and spirit. Most Christian bookstores either stock the book or can order it.

The soul is the determining factor of our being. God didn't create us to be robots that blindly follow his leading. He gave us the freedom of choice, a free will. The spirit can only act on the body through the soul. This sovereign power allows us to make a free choice to follow the will of God, the will of Satan, and even our own will. The soul decides whether the spiritual world or the natural world will reign in the individual. God's plan and original perfect design is that the soul would take instruction from the spirit which is in communication with God's spirit. This was how Adam was originally designed and created.

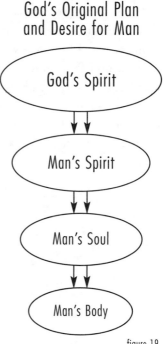

God's Original Plan and Desire for Man

God's Spirit

Man's Spirit

Man's Soul

Man's Body

figure 19

Figure 19 shows God's intended order with our spirit connected to and taking direction from God's Spirit. The soul being under the direction of our spirit relates with and directs the physical body. This is God's design for the proper chain of command.

Many of us know the story of what happened to Adam and Eve. God gave Adam and Eve the authority to rule over his entire creation on earth. He gave them charge over everything. Because he created each individual to have free will it was necessary to provide a way for us to exercise that free will. So he placed Adam and Eve in the Garden of Eden and told them they could eat of everything in the garden except for the tree in the middle of the garden, the Tree of the Knowledge of Good and Evil. God provided Adam and Eve with the choice to obey or not to obey his command, and he even warned Adam of the consequences of making the wrong choice, which was death (Genesis 2:17).

Adam and Eve exercised their free will, and with a little deception thrown in from the serpent (Satan), they disobeyed God and ate from the Tree of the Knowledge of Good and Evil. Obviously they didn't drop dead immediately. They both lived to be hundreds of years old. So was God kidding when he told them they would die? Not really. Their action forced him to separate his Spirit from them. In other words, the nature of his relationship with the crown jewel of his creation changed in an instant. We will see in the next chapter what this meant for Adam and Eve and for the rest of humankind.

CHAPTER 11

A Case of the Tail Wagging the Dog!

Here we continue the story after Adam and Eve disobeyed God and ate from the Tree of the Knowledge of Good and Evil. God's perfect nature could no longer associate with them because they had become infected with the sin of disobedience. And so he detached his Spirit from Adam and Eve, in effect, making them dead to him; thus the "surely you will die." (They eventually did die physically as well).

Because they had gained the knowledge of good and evil, their condition would be passed down to their children and to all people thereafter. Figures 20 and 21 show the progression of what happened after Adam and Eve became separated from their ideal relationship with God. With the spirit of man no longer in communion with God, the soul of man became the dominant factor. After Adam and Eve sinned against God their soul no longer took direction from God through the spirit.

Without this direct pipeline to God through the spirit, the soul is left with three alternatives: to be led by the sensual body with its lusts and cravings (Figure 22); to connect its spirit to another spirit (we see this in those who worship Satan through a cult) (Figure 23);

God's Separation from Man

Man's Spirit No Longer the Dominant Factor

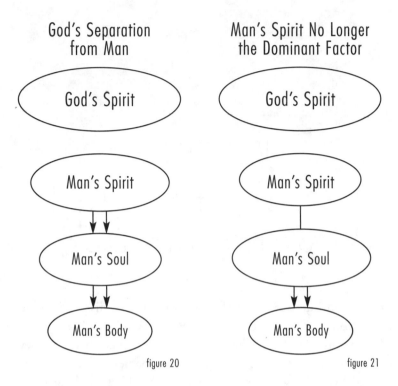

figure 20   figure 21

or the soul becomes the controlling factor itself, led by the mind, will, and emotions (Figure 21). At different times the dominant factor can alternate between our body, soul, and spirit. In any case, the soul becomes overdeveloped as it continues to exercise free will apart from God. The soul becomes puffed up, so to speak. Every person after Adam and Eve is born separated from God's Spirit.

So what does all this mean for you and me? We are born separated from God and into a sinful world. Because our soul with its mind, will, and emotions is in charge, we often become the product of our upbringing, our learned responses, abuses, faulty self-concepts, the opinions of others, negative influences, selfish ambitions, the love of money, our addictions, our lusts and cravings, forces of evil, etc. The list goes on and on. It becomes impossible for us to be whole and healthy because of all the baggage we carry. Can you see how a life separated from God leads to an unhealthy life with all its problems?

It is impossible for us to experience true physical health without being healthy in soul and spirit!

The Bible also warns us that a life apart from God eventually leads to death! "What good is it for a man to gain the whole world, yet forfeit his soul?" (Mark 8:36)

Have you ever been in a public setting and seen someone's child throw an absolute tantrum? Then you watch as the parent tries very nicely to beg, plead, and implore the child to stop misbehaving, without any success. This happens in my office on occasion, and I usually tell my staff, "That was another case of the tail wagging the dog!" When our spirit is disconnected from God's Spirit, the tail is wagging the dog!

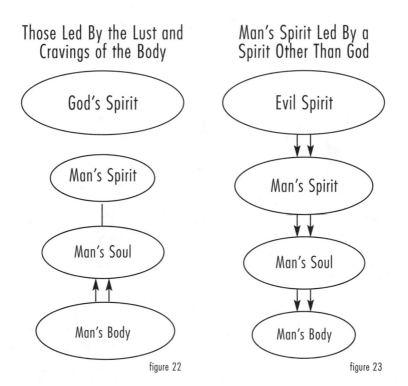

Those Led By the Lust and Cravings of the Body

God's Spirit

Man's Spirit

Man's Soul

Man's Body

figure 22

Man's Spirit Led By a Spirit Other Than God

Evil Spirit

Man's Spirit

Man's Soul

Man's Body

figure 23

CHAPTER 12

Mission Impossible?

The mission should we choose to accept it is this: To join our spirit with God's Spirit to restore communication with God. The mission is complicated by the fact that our spirit, the only way to communicate with God, is malfunctioning; it is useless. The only tool we have to work with is our soul (mind, will, emotions), but our soul can't comprehend God and is unable to restore this much needed communication. Sound like an impossible mission? Let's look at this mission from our perspective and then from God's to see if there is a way to accomplish this mission.

From our perspective there is a huge hurdle to overcome in accomplishing this mission. The hurdle is our inability to comprehend God even if we want to. A recent experience highlights this obstacle. A few years ago I purchased a property for investment on a beautiful lake in northern Minnesota. I was able to subdivide the property into three parcels, two very nice lake lots and one wooded lot with unusual terrain that was loaded with underbrush. I knew it would make a nice lot for a small house or cabin because I could picture what the lot would look like without the heavy underbrush. In essence, I had a vision for the possibilities for this property. When I listed the property with a real estate agent, we assumed it would sell rather quickly because of the demand for this type of property. But the property was shown once or twice a week for over six months without an offer. It was perplexing to me, and the only thing I could think of was that the people looking at the property must not be able to see the potential for this property. I decided to hire a company to clear the underbrush from the building site which created a nice view of the lake. The property sold three days later! In the same way the people viewing this property needed help to see its potential before they were willing to purchase it, we need help to be able to see God. It is impossible for us to do so on our own. We need someone to clear the underbrush so we can see. The people looking at this property wanted to see the potential, but they just simply couldn't. I believe this lack of vision is especially true in America, where the high standard of living has created a jungle of underbrush, blocking our view of God and even the perception of our need for him.

In examining this mission from God's perspective, imagine for a moment that you are him. You made people to be like you, with intellect, emotions, and a spirit so they could relate to you like a child connects with a benevolent father. You love them and gave them everything they could ever want. But you also allowed these people to have a will of their own because you didn't want a one sided relationship; you didn't want robots. Of course, Adam and Eve let you down by disobeying the one simple command that you gave them, and so infecting the entire population thereafter.

You love people dearly and want to have a relationship with them, but you just can't tarnish your perfect nature with their disobedience called sin. You have to eradicate sin and those who house it. You also know that they can't do anything to solve their situation. What would you do? How would you resolve this dilemma? I have pondered the idea many times, and I don't believe it is possible to come up with a better plan for solving this seemingly impossible mission than the one God has executed.

Here is the amazing plan that God chose to accomplish this mission. God himself is three dimensional consisting of Father, Son, and Holy Spirit. So he sent his Son, whom we know as Jesus

Christ, to live here on earth with us; he was the only man to live here and never sin. Because he was without sin, he was uniquely qualified to serve as a substitute to pay the penalty (death) for our sin so that we could have a restored relationship with God. A friend of mine describes it like this:

"Jesus paid a debt that he didn't owe to cover
a debt we couldn't pay."

God loves his creation so much that he sacrificed his own Son so that we could have a restored relationship with him. This restored relationship is crucial because it guarantees that we will have a life with God in heaven even after we die here on earth. It also helps us to experience healing and have a better life in the short time we are here on earth. Look at these promises given to us in the Bible:

"For God so loved the world that he gave his one
and only Son, that whoever believes in him
shall not perish but have eternal life."

JOHN 3:16

"The thief comes only to steal and kill and
destroy; I have come that they may have life,
and have it to the full."

JOHN 10:10

Here is the most amazing thing. God's perfect plan for accomplishing this mission is so easy it can be accomplished by a child; and yet it still allows us to exercise our freedom of choice! God simply asks us to acknowledge our separation, admit our faults (our sinful life) and simply believe that Jesus Christ paid the price for our sinful condition, and then we will be saved, and our spirit joined with God's Spirit. It's that simple and yet it can be so difficult.

In my experience, there are two groups of people who are the most likely to exercise their free will and accept this free gift from God: 1) Children, because they haven't been overly hardened by the stresses of life, and they find it easier to believe, and 2) Those in crisis. When things are going well, we often don't feel the need for God. When I hear personal testimonies of those who have accepted God's gift of salvation, I most often hear of a personal crisis that led them to cry out to God for help. On a recent mission trip to a developing country, I was amazed at the percentage of those who accepted Jesus as Lord of their life when we shared the Good News, but they were a people with much need. Please understand that you don't have to fall into either of these two categories to accept Christ as your savior. I mention this so it may open your eyes as to why you or others are not receptive to God's plan for salvation.

*This and the next caution point out the most likely "underbrush" of preconceived ideas that can prevent you from experiencing the "Aha Moment" necessary to accomplish the mission in the only way offered by God. This first caution may apply to some of the 60 % who claim a belief in the God described in the Bible. As you have been reading this chapter you may be saying to yourself, "I'm already saved. I have been a good _____ (insert Catholic, Lutheran, Baptist, Methodist, Presbyterian, or any other Christian religion!) for a long time." You must know that going to church regularly doesn't make you a Christian! This may be offensive to some reading this, but religion is different than a personal relationship with God. Residing in a garage doesn't make you a car! Jesus told Nicodemus, a **religious leader**, that he needed to be born again to be saved. In the same way, baptism, first communion, and confirmation will not restore a relation-*

ship with God. Becoming a Christian requires that you earnestly come to God, confess your sinful condition, believe that Jesus died for that sin, that he rose from the dead, and accept Jesus as the Savior that he is. Only then will you be set free from your burdens and begin healing, and have eternal life with God.

My goal here is not to cause doubt about your belief in God, but for you to be certain of your relationship with God. Perhaps my favorite passage from the Bible may help you to understand more clearly:

In the year that King Uzziah died, I (Isaiah) saw the Lord seated on a
throne, high and exalted, and the train of his robe filled the temple.
Above him were seraphs, each with six wings: With two wings
they covered their faces, with two they covered their feet, and
with two they were flying. And they were calling to one another:
"Holy, holy, holy is the LORD Almighty;
the whole earth is full of his glory."
At the sound of their voices the doorposts and thresholds shook and the
temple was filled with smoke. "Woe to me!" I cried. "I am ruined!
For I am a man of unclean lips, and I live among a people of unclean
lips, and my eyes have seen the King, the LORD Almighty."
Then one of the seraphs flew to me with a live coal in his hand,
which he had taken with tongs from the altar. With it he touched
my mouth and said, "See, this has touched your lips; your guilt
is taken away and your sin atoned for."
Then I heard the voice of the Lord saying, "Whom shall I send?
And who will go for us?" And I said, "Here am I. Send me!"

ISAIAH 6:1-8

In this passage we find Isaiah, a respected leader in his faith community, in an unexpected face-to-face encounter with God. Notice his first words: "Woe to me! I am ruined! For I am a man of unclean lips and I live among a people of unclean lips...." Prior to this encounter, Isaiah probably thought he was doing just fine as a prophet for God, but suddenly standing in the presence of a pure, loving, and holy God gave him a realization of his own sinful condition. At that moment he wasn't thinking about what a good church-goer he had been. He really thought he was going to die. He was totally at God's mercy. Have you ever experienced God's love in such a way that you realized your sinful condition and knew you needed his mercy? The good news for Isaiah is that God provided a way for his sins to be forgiven. Our Good News is Jesus Christ.

Maybe you haven't had a God experience like Isaiah, and after reading this are even more uncertain of your relationship with God. The Bible tells us we can know Christians by their fruit. In other words, you should notice steady changes in your life towards Christ-likeness once you are on God's team. Take stock of the last two-five years of your life. Do you have more love, peace, and joy? Do you love God more now than you did a few years ago? Do you love your wife more, your children more, and your boss more? Have you forgiven someone who has hurt you deeply? Do you have more purpose and more awareness of God's plan for you? After Isaiah was touched by God he answered the call by saying, "Here am I. Send me!" Where is God sending you?

If your heart is being pricked by these words; if you suddenly feel unsettled, God is probably ringing your phone right now. Maybe its time to pick up the phone and answer God's call for the first real time in your life. I was a part of the church for years before I picked up the phone and answered the call from God.

Perhaps you're one of the 40 % of Americans who don't profess a belief in the God described in the Bible. You've just read this chapter and are saying, "I still don't buy this stuff. I thought

this was a book about truth, about facts. None of these things he writes about God and Jesus are based on science and fact. It's all just conjecture from one religious perspective!" The purpose of this book isn't to change your mind, but to state the truth. It is your choice to accept it or not.

As stated earlier, the gap between faith in God and scientific evidence of the existence of God is closing. The scientific knowledge gained in just the past fifty years has shot serious holes in Darwin's Theory of Evolution and natural selection. When you better understand some of these implications, you will find that it takes more faith to be an atheist (one who doesn't believe in the existence of God) or an agnostic (one who neither accepts nor rejects the existence of God) than to believe in God.

Let's just say this: If what I have said is true then this becomes a life and death issue. Please don't just hang on to your preconceived ideas without further investigation. Go get the two books written by Lee Strobel I cited in Chapter 9. Another good book is "Evidence that Demands a Verdict," written by Josh McDowell. Or simply dust off the Bible you may have received as a child and open it up to the book of John. Maybe God wants to speak to you directly! The claims made about Jesus Christ in the Bible (along with other historical evidence) leave us with only three possible conclusions: Either Jesus was a liar, a lunatic, or Savior of the World. It is imperative that you know for sure what the right answer is because it will determine your place in eternity!

If you are ready to begin an exciting adventure with God right now, please go to a quiet place, get down on your knees and pray these words with me right now. Speak them out loud to God! When you do, here's what God promises in return: "If you confess with your mouth, "Jesus is Lord," and believe in your heart that God raised Him from the dead, you will be saved." (Romans 10:9)

Dear Lord, I give up, I surrender!
I'm tired of living life my own way, apart from you.
I'm tired of being tossed around by my mind, will, and emotions
which have been beaten up by past abuses, let downs,
selfishness, faulty self-image, and misconceptions.
I want to change my situation, but I need your help.
Forgive me for trying to live life on my own.
Forgive me for all my sins.
Forgive me for the hurts I have caused others,
especially the ones I love. I accept the gift you offer.
I give my life to you. I believe that Jesus died to pay the price
for my sin, and I ask you to be Lord of my life. Amen.

Mission Accomplished! But the adventure has just begun. Oh, and by the way, go tell someone. God likes that!

CHAPTER 13

The Connection!

In this chapter I want to briefly explain what happens when our spirit reconnects to God. But before I begin, if you just earnestly shared the previous prayer with God, let me congratulate you on the beginning of your new life with God!

"What this means is that those who become Christians become new persons. They are not the same anymore, for the old life is gone. A new life has begun! All this newness of life is from God, who brought us back to himself through what Christ did. And God has given us the task of reconciling people to him."

2 CORINTHIANS 5:17-18 (NLT)

You may recall that prior to the acceptance of the gift of salvation through Jesus Christ, our spirit is dead to God. At the moment we accept Christ, God quickens our spirit. "To quicken" means to bring to life something that was previously dead. This is the job of the Holy Spirit. When we accept Christ as our Savior, God's Holy Spirit joins with our spirit, supernaturally reviving it, so to speak. This is like tuning in a radio into the signal source, the radio station. The Holy Spirit enables our spirit to have clear communication with God. At the moment of this quickening, our spirit is instantly made right with God. It is in the spirit that our new life spoken about above begins.

Our soul, however, is another story. Our mind, will, and emotions aren't changed by God in an instant like our spirit. Because our soul is the instrument for expressing our life and personality, and because it has been in charge of our life for so long, changes here come more slowly as our spirit slowly regains its rightful influence over the soul. The Bible describes the process like this:

"Do not conform any longer to the pattern of this world,
but be transformed by the renewing of your mind.
Then you will be able to test and approve what God's will is—
his good, pleasing and perfect will."

ROMANS 12:2

This is a process whereby we become more like Christ as we mature in our life as a believer. So in other words even though we are saved, sometimes we don't act like it. However, evidence of a new life with God is that we allow the Holy Spirit to change us over time so that we become mature Christians. Figure 24 shows a life reconnected to God and the change that occurs as the soul gradually cedes authority and control to the spirit.

When we are first saved (born again) the Bible tells us we are like babies, unable to care for ourselves. We need other, more mature, Christians to care for us and help

Salvation and the Process of Sanctification

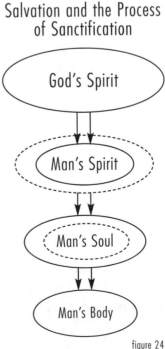

figure 24

us in our new life. This is the job of the church. Many people think of the church as just a building, but the church is really other believers. In the past, you may have been hurt by people or leaders in the church. Because the church is made up of people who, like you, are in the process of becoming more like Christ with time, they are not perfect. So be patient; many well-meaning Christians make mistakes that hurt and cause confusion in new believers.

If you are not part of a church family already, find a church that is based foremost on sound biblical teaching and that fits with your tastes and personality. Then make a commitment to stick with it! Again, your relationship with the church is much like a child-parent relationship. No parents are perfect, but a child is usually only removed from a home if there is abuse that threatens the mental or physical well-being of the child. Also, don't forget that you will go through an adolescent phase of your spiritual maturity, and the temptation to become rebellious and run away from home may present itself.

Finally, I recommend two books: The *Quest Study Bible* (Zondervan) because it provides answers in the margins to many common questions that arise during reading; and *The Purpose Driven Life (Zondervan)* written by Rick Warren because this book will help you to live the life that God intends. Pastor Warren has done a masterful job at summing up key incites I have drawn from hundreds of other books and packaged them up in one easy reading book.

Besides the promise of a life with God in heaven, a relationship with God through Christ brings physical, spiritual, mental, and emotional healing during our short time here on earth. The believer now has the ability to enlist the power of God Almighty in problem solving, conflict resolution, physical healing, and changing unwanted habits. Pastor Jim Sky, my friend mentioned earlier, sums up the life in Christ like this: "For those who have accepted Christ their spirit is healed, their soul is being healed, and their body will be healed." The change of mind and will necessary to take responsibility for the five key areas of our health are now possible as we gain the mind and heart of the Lord through our spirit and as our soul assumes its rightful place in submission to the Spirit. God is for us and wants only the best for us:

"'For I know the plans I have for you,'" declares the Lord,
"'plans to prosper you and not to harm you,
plans to give you hope and a future.'"

JEREMIAH 29:11

"And we know that in all things God works for the good of
those who love him, who have been called according to his purpose."

ROMANS 8:28

The child of God can accept responsibility for health and begin to tackle challenges with the confidence knowing that with Christ, all things are possible!

CHAPTER 14

Can I Get a Witness?

Throughout this book I have shared bits and pieces of my personal struggles with my own health. In this last chapter I want to share the rest of my story with the hope that it will encourage and spur you on to achieve the desire of your heart.

Why Can't I Be Like...? This was me as a child. When I was a young boy I used to think that everybody was normal except me and my family. My mom became pregnant with me when she was seventeen. To support his new family while struggling to get through college, my dad worked multiple jobs and was not home much when I was young. Mom struggled with loneliness, the stress of having two young kids to care for (my sister came along ten months after me) as well as a lot of baggage she carried from her own childhood abuses.

As we got older, I always remember my sister getting into trouble at school and at home. There always seemed to be problems with something, usually either money or family. There were times when I overheard loud discussions between mom and dad about some of these problems. My mom's drinking turned to alcoholism and the entire family suffered the effects of this for many years. I wet the bed at night until I was fifteen. I always felt my dad was emotionally detached from us. I found it difficult to know sometimes if he approved of me or how much he even loved me. Deep down I was pretty sure he did, but his stoic Norwegian personality wouldn't lend itself to statements like, "I love you."

We moved at least a half-dozen times when I was young so I never developed any lasting friendships. I was never really liked in school and kept to myself a lot. I did have a lot of great times as a child, and I remember many positive experiences with my family, but I can't tell you how many times I used to wish that our family could be more like the neighbors or some of my relatives. They seemed to be so "normal" and happy, and our family seemed to be so messed up.

As the oldest child in this alcoholic home I became the fixer. I coped with the situation by becoming an overachiever. I excelled in academics, was pretty good in sports, and I spent lots of energy trying to make others happy. I became a perfectionist and found the incessant need to be right. Deep down inside however, I felt like I never measured up. Almost on a daily basis I had to assess the situation with my mom. At any given time I had to determine if she was drunk, hung-over, sad, or happy. In doing so, I became very good at assessing people's tone level and their attitudes towards me. Of course, my first taste of alcohol when I was in eighth grade (seven cans of beer) started me on a path of drowning my insecurities. I learned how to drink to get drunk very early and added cigarettes when I was seventeen.

After my first year of college, the twenty foot fall from the ladder I previously mentioned set my career path. I am very mechanically minded and so when the chiropractor explained my problem in a way that made perfect sense to my analytical mind, I knew I would become a chiropractor. But it wasn't until years later that I discovered the real reason why I became a chiropractor was to fill a huge emotional need. You see, when I sat for the first time in the waiting room of this very busy office I immediately picked up on the attitudes of the others waiting to be seen. They sat there quiet, reserved, with no eye contact, no smiles and their faces buried in magazines.

In contrast, I noticed the patients who returned to the reception area after seeing the doctor were much different. They were jovial, pleasantly conversing, they seemed much happier, and had a much higher energy level. I had never experienced this in the medical doctor's office. People usually walked out of those offices the same way they had walked in. My keen awareness to this change in tone levels alerted the fixer inside of me that being a chiropractor would allow me to do something I had never been able to do at home, change someone's tone level.

Once this career path was set I was very driven to succeed and decided I was not going to let anything stop me from my goal. I remember assuring my dad that I wasn't going to allow a woman to slow or derail my career plans in the same way that had caused my folks to struggle. I met the girl of my dreams, Lisa, three weeks later. I portrayed a lot of confidence, an attitude of success and of course I showered her with attention. I tried very hard not to let her see the dark side of my family, and I did a pretty good job of hiding many of my insecurities. Once however, I remember her concern because she didn't feel like she could have an opinion of her own, and she felt she was never right around me. I assured her that everything would be fine and that I would work on this area.

Our relationship continued to grow, and we married during my first year of chiropractic school in Atlanta. Of course it didn't take her long to realize that the man she married was not the same man she had dated. (This was even true physically because I gained over fifty pounds in our first year of marriage after I quit smoking and processed foods became a staple in my diet). I was always right, and she was always wrong. I became very jealous of anything she wanted to do that didn't include me. Deep down I was afraid that I would lose her now that she knew the real me. I became very controlling and short tempered. When she tried to talk to anyone about our marriage and her concerns about me, I totally shut her down. Just as with my ancestors, family problems are private problems! Drinking became a regular part of my routine. We received an entire case of Jack Daniels Whiskey as a wedding present and I drank it in less than eight months. Lisa and I had some fun times during those early years. I played college rugby and that experience enabled us to see much of the southeastern US. During these years I did many things to harm my body, not to mention my marriage.

After graduation we moved back home and rented (very cheaply) a small house from my mom and dad that was near theirs. By this time I had started smoking again. Now Lisa was six months pregnant with our son Matt. I didn't

Beer by the Pitcherr

find out until years later, but I was treating Lisa so badly that first year back home that my mom even offered to have her come and live with them for awhile. All this time I was blind to the offenses and protective walls that were piling up in the woman I loved. Things became easier for Lisa once we started having children because she could pour her energies into being a mom. She pulled away from me emotionally so gradually that I'm not sure either one of us realized it.

Meanwhile, I continued to pour my energies into becoming a success. We opened our own clinic on a shoe-string budget, and we eked by for the first few years. Slowly but surely, the practice grew and after nearly ten years of marriage, we purchased our first house. Surely a new house would make me happy. Soon after the house came a new four-wheel-drive pickup, then the new boat. I measured success and happiness by our economic status. And I was always hungry for more. I can still remember the let down that followed each new purchase when I realized it didn't really satisfy me, but I kept trying.

Status was also very important for me. When I became involved in any organization I usually rose to the top. I joined the Jaycees and within a year I was president. I was appointed to the Minnesota Board of Chiropractic Examiners and within a year became president. I joined a local church and was president of the council within a few years. The local Chamber of Commerce had plans for me to be president after a short period of time. I remember the short-lived elation at being honored as one of the "Ten Outstanding Young Minnesotans" by the Minnesota Jaycees.

My church life was out of obligation. It was the right thing to do. I grew up in the Lutheran Church. Like the other kids, I memorized the Catechism and the books of the Bible during my two years of Confirmation. But I never sensed approval from God. I always felt like he was this big judge in the sky looking down to see if I was doing it good enough, but yet he would never tell me. (Our view of God often parallels our view of our father). My wife and I attended church regularly especially after we had children. I taught Sunday school, sat on the board, and sang in the choir because it was the right thing to do.

By this time, I figured I had worked hard enough to become like those neighbors and relatives I had admired during my youth. The bad habits of my younger days were pretty much under control. I never drank more than two drinks if I had to see patients the following day. I rarely drank to get plastered, but the few drinks in the evening sure helped me to check out emotionally after a long day of seeing patients. My marriage was a little better than in the early years. I had softened a little bit with age, but by this time Lisa's walls were so high I couldn't hurt her much anyway. I continued to feel resentment at the love and attention she poured out on our kids, feeling like I was getting the table scraps of her affections. I knew I still wasn't happy, but I figured it wouldn't get much better than this.

Then in 1992 my life turned upside down. For about a year, Don Ratzlaff, a member of our church had been pestering Lisa and me to attend a church retreat for married couples. It was organized in such a way that husbands attend the three day retreat one weekend and wives attend the following weekend. In October we finally relented. I remember feeling so helpless and out of control of the situation as Don and his wife Marion dropped me off at a church about an hour away from my house. This meant that I couldn't leave even if I wanted to.

It is very difficult to explain what happened to me during this retreat except to say that I experienced God's love for the first time in my life. I realized that all my preconceived ideas about God were wrong and that I had never really known the God that is described in the Bible. I had only seen a Lutheran/Johnson hybrid. I surrendered that weekend and asked Jesus to be Lord of my life.

Don and Marion brought home a different man. My wife was a little nervous to go the following weekend because I was acting so weird. She told Don and Marion that they had brought home a different man. It turned out okay because she ended up having a similar experience (her previous understanding of God was a Catholic/Lang hybrid).

The feeling for me was one of incredible relief. The pressure and weight of trying to measure up all those years was gone. The Lord had somehow released me from all my stresses, shortcomings, and burdens. I immediately stopped swearing. My temper was tempered. I became less selfish. All of our friends kept asking what happened to me.

I realized that all of my years of church going hadn't made me a Christian. I resided in the garage but wasn't really a car! It was that moment in 1992 when I surrendered my life to Jesus, that God met me face to face and changed me. A few months later I experienced the Holy Spirit in a very real way and knew from that moment on that my spirit had indeed been inhabited by the Spirit of the Living God. Deep down in my core was God's deposit of perfect love!

God has been very patient with me. It has taken years to change many of my character flaws, faulty self-concepts, and the many sinful areas of my life. I am not perfect, just saved. With God's grace I have learned how to give my wife the love I could never give her before but which she deserves. It has taken years for us to dismantle those protective walls Lisa put up in our early years and for me to replace the kids as the love of her life.

Our marriage is a testament to the power of God and his mercy (also the mercy of Lisa early in our marriage and her commitment to her vows). Both of our children, Matt and Beth, love the Lord. I receive comments all the time from people who cross paths with them and are amazed at the kindness and love they both demonstrate. I am so grateful to the Lord for changing my heart while our children were still fairly young and at home. In fact, most of my family has given their life to Christ, having seen God's work in us.

God's work will never be finished while I am on this earth. But I want to share a particular battle that gives testimony to the healing power of God. Several years back, I had been seeking and at the same time wrestling with God for several months over my alcohol consumption. Even though I only consumed a few drinks each sitting and limited myself to two or three nights a week, I knew deep down that I was addicted. I just didn't want to quit. It became a great way to check out emotionally after the stress of being a doctor all day. I know enough about alcoholism to know if you need to drink, you are hooked. I also became concerned because my habit of "checking out" excluded my wife and children from my life during those times (Just give me the TV remote and leave me alone). I also desired to break the generational curse of alcoholism that ran in my family.

One particular evening I invited another doctor in my office to a Christian conference so that he might respond to Christ through the words of a well known speaker. The keynote speaker shared for about an hour and a half. It was a great talk about the claims of

Americans as believers in God and yet we have more social problems such as divorce, suicide, drug and alcohol abuse, etc., than anyplace else in the entire world. He laid out a challenge for us to live the victorious Christian life we are claiming and then invited us up to the altar.

I hadn't thought about my drinking the entire night, but I was moved by his words so I went forward. When I knelt down, the instant my knees touched the floor I had a tremendously vivid recollection of how much I detested alcohol as a child. It was as if I was suddenly ten years old again and crying about my mom's drinking. I couldn't recall ever having a thought like this since I had started drinking myself. In that instant, God took the taste for alcohol away from me, and I haven't consumed alcohol since that night in August of 2000. At that time, Matt and Beth, were thirteen and fourteen years old, the age when peer pressure to drink was just mounting. I thank God for his timing and that neither of my children have the desire to consume alcohol.

I kicked a ten year smoking habit several years ago. As I said earlier, my highest weight has been 328 pounds On August 24, 2005 I weighed in at 228 pounds (see picture). With continued help from the Lord I will reach my goal of 210 pounds. Diet plans don't usually bring permanent results but God's healing does!

The Johnson Famiily

These are just a few examples of God's grace and mercy shown to me and my family since that weekend in 1992. I could write another book giving witness to the other healing work of God in my life, in my family's life and in the people I know, but I wish to close by telling you about my parents.

As I get older I realize just how blessed I am to have parents who didn't take the easy way out, but loved me, took responsibility to raise me, and honored their commitment to marriage "for better or for worse." I also realize that what I thought was a rather dysfunctional family is really rather typical for most families who don't understand who God really is and make Him a daily part of their homes. I have since come to find out that those friends and relatives, who I wished we could be more like, had many serious problems of their own. In fact, compared to some of the dysfunction I see in families today, I am even more grateful for my parents.

Mom quit drinking during my first year of college after crying out to God for help during her treatment program. My dad gave his life to Christ several years back and today we rarely end a conversion without saying, "I love you." Sure, my dad sacrificed time with us when we were little so that he could provide for us, but as I got older he sure made up for it. For much of my teenage years, we were inseparable. I have lots of great memories of our backyard projects, our hunting and fishing trips as well as other times that make me realize just how blessed I am to have such a caring and loving dad. Thanks mom and dad for giving me the best you could give with what you had and for allowing God to change you into awesome people!

Well, there you have it, the necessary ingredients for a healthy life. Merriam-Webster has indeed properly defined health as *the condition of being sound in body, mind, and spirit.* I encourage you to look again at Webster's definition of the word whole. Nearly all of the definitions describe the life that is found in Jesus Christ. If you have openly and honestly cried out, "I'm sick and tired of being sick and tired!"

He has heard you and is ready to begin eating that elephant with you. He'll help you and hold your hand like a friend if you let him. If I don't see you sooner, I hope to see you in heaven!

I pray that from his glorious, unlimited resources
he will give you mighty inner strength through his Holy Spirit.
And I pray that Christ will be more and more at home
in your heart as you trust in him.
May your inner roots go down deep into
the soil of God's marvelous love.
And may you have the power to understand,
as all God's people should,
how wide, how long, how high and how deep
his love really is.
May you experience the love of Christ,
though it is so great you will never really understand it.
Then you will be filled with the fullness of life
and power that comes from God.

EPHESIANS 3:16-19 (NLT)

Epilogue

How I Ate the Elephant

The Bible speaks of fasting and prayer while seeking the Lord. When I began this book I fasted for forty days. During this time I consumed nothing but juice prepared with a juicer from fresh, organic fruits and vegetables, along with a mineral broth and a multivitamin/mineral formula. In essence, I addressed the "four elephants in the middle of my room" (portion size, sugar, processed foods and drugs/alcohol) all at the same time. At the end of the forty days, I felt great. I lost 30+ pounds, my resting blood pressure dropped from 138/88 to 126/68 and my heart rate went from 85 to 65 beats per minute. Several other little annoying health issues seemed to clear up during this time as well.

When I was sharing my fasting experience with a family member who works with computers, he said, "It sounds like you rebooted your body." It was a great description for what I believed happened to my body. I had cleansed and detoxified my body, enabling it to function as it was designed. Am I suggesting a forty day juice fast is the solution for your health problems? Not at all! Without direct supervision by a doctor prolonged fasting can be dangerous.

The improvement was short-lived anyway because I returned to my old eating habits after the fast. It didn't take long to gain back much of my original weight and notice some of the old familiar symptoms returning. But as I spent more and more time doing research for the chapter on nutrition, the Lord began to work another miracle in me. As I sought him more diligently, he began to take away the desire and cravings for bad food.

My wife and I attended a healthy cooking class, and we began to replace many unhealthy foods in our house with organic, whole foods. Since then I have markedly reduced the amount of refined sugar and trans fats in my diet. In addition I have cut back on portion sizes considerably, and if I want that evening bowl of ice cream I run some frozen bananas and peaches through my juicer and enjoy a great treat. My friends even come over for my ice cream!

I ride my bicycle in the summer and cross-country ski in the winter. I try hard to maintain a normal sleep schedule. And of course, the Lord has given me peace and contentment. As Lisa and I have considered what really matters in our life, we are learning to enjoy a simpler life with fewer material possesions. We enjoy making a difference in the workplace and in our community. The Lord has healed our marriage to the point where we now lead a course for married couples at our church. I still experience discipline from the Lord when pride or other stuff gets in the way of my relationship with him. This is good because the Bible tells us, "the Lord disciplines those he loves."

My success in the area of nutrition was simply a combination of recognizing the elephants in my life, trusting God to help me push them out of the room, and patience. I believe as you seek the Lord for help, he will lead you in the way he wants to heal you. He will show you where and how to begin with your elephant(s)! He has been working on me since 1992, "one bite at a time." You see, it is the Lord who is getting rid of my *elephants*, not me. Put your trust in him, and He'll do the same. It's that easy!

Glossary

Definitions from Merriam-Webster's Online Dictionary (www.m-w.com)

Main Entry: **health**

Pronunciation: 'helth *also* 'heltth

Function: *noun*

Usage: *often attributive*

Etymology: Middle English *helthe,* from Old English *h[AE]lth,* from *hAl*

1 a : the condition of being sound in body, mind, or spirit; *especially* : freedom from physical disease or pain **b** : the general condition of the body <in poor *health*> <enjoys good *health*>

2 a : flourishing condition : **WELL-BEING** <defending the *health* of the beloved oceans — Peter Wilkinson> **b** : general condition or state <poor economic *health*>

3 : a toast to someone's health or prosperity (1)

Main Entry: **truth**

Pronunciation: 'trüth

Function: *noun*

Inflected Form(s): *plural* **truths** /'trü[th]z, 'trüths/

Etymology: Middle English *trewthe,* from Old English *trEowth* fidelity; akin to Old English *trEowe* faithful — more at TRUE

1 a *archaic* : **FIDELITY, CONSTANCY b** : sincerity in action, character, and utterance
2 a (1) : the state of being the case : **FACT** (2) : the body of real things, events, and facts : **ACTUALITY** (3) *often capitalized* : a transcendent fundamental or spiritual reality **b** : a judgment, proposition, or idea that is true or accepted as true <*truths* of thermodynamics> **c** : the body of true statements and propositions
3 a : the property (as of a statement) of being in accord with fact or reality **b** *chiefly British* : **TRUE** 2 **c** : fidelity to an original or to a standard
4 *capitalized, Christian Science* : **GOD**
- **in truth :** in accordance with fact : **ACTUALLY** (3)

Main Entry: **¹whole**
Pronunciation: 'hOl
Function: *adjective*
Etymology: Middle English *hool* healthy, unhurt, entire, from Old English *hAl;* akin to Old High German *heil* healthy, unhurt, Old Norse *heill,* Old Church Slavonic *celu*
1 a (1) : free of wound or injury : UNHURT (2) : recovered from a wound or injury : RESTORED (3) : being healed <*whole* of an ancient evil, I sleep sound — A. E. Housman> **b** : free of defect or impairment : INTACT **c** : physically sound and healthy : free of disease or deformity **d** : mentally or emotionally sound
2 : having all its proper parts or components : COMPLETE, UNMODIFIED <*whole* milk> <a *whole* egg>
3 a : constituting the total sum or undiminished entirety : ENTIRE <owns the *whole* island> **b** : each or all of the <took part in the *whole* series of athletic events>
4 a : constituting an undivided unit : UNBROKEN, UNCUT <a *whole* roast suckling pig> **b** : directed to one end : CONCENTRATED <promised to give it his *whole* attention>
5 a : seemingly complete or total <the *whole* idea is to help, not hinder> **b** : very great in quantity, extent, or scope <feels a *whole* lot better now>
6 : constituting the entirety of a person's nature or development <educate the

Need to check accuracy of pages after typesetting is complete.
Is picture placement on the page corrected in typesetting?

References

[i] Center for Medicare & Medicaid Services, CMS News, Thursday, January 8, 2004.

[ii] D.M. Eisenberg, Annals of Internal Medicine, July 1997.

[iii] National Center for Health Statistics, Chart Book on Trends in the Health of Americans, 2003.

[iv] Lucas JW, Schiller JS, Benson V. Summary health statistics for U.S. Adults: National Health Interview Survey, 2001. National Center for Health Statistics.

Vital Health Stat 10(218), 2004.

[v] National Sleep Foundation, How Sleepy Are You? 1999 Sleep Survey Shows Disturbing Trends in Daytime Sleepiness, 1999; www.sleepfoundation.org.

[vi] Guyton AC, Textbook of Medical Physiology, W.B. Saunders Company, 1991.

[vii] Merriam Webster Inc., Merriam-Webster Online Dictionary, www.m-w.com, search the word—homeostasis, 2004.

[viii] Stephen E. Strauss, MD, director of NCCAM; Richard L. Nahin, PhD, MPH, senior advisor for Scientific Coordination and Outreach, NCCAM; "Complementary and Alternative Medicine Use Among Adults: United States, 2002.

[ix] Merriam Webster Inc., Merriam-Webster Online Dictionary, www.m-w.com, search the word—alignment and balance, 2004.

[x] Seeman DC. Anatometer Measurements: A Field Study Intra– and Inter-Examiner Reliability and Pre to Post Changes Following an Atlas Adjustment. Chiropractic Research Journal, 1999; 6(1):7-9.

[xi] Basmajian, MD. Muscles and Movements, 1977, Referenced in A.U.C.C.O. Journal, Chiropractic in the Twenty First Century – VECTOR, Vol. 2 –No. 4, Fall 1999.

[xii] Gregory, R, The Upper Cervical Monograph, Vol. 1 – No. 7, page 3, May 1975.

[xiii] Murphy, D, Lecture Notes, NUCCA Conference, Nov. 2004.

[xiv] Lennon J, et al. Postural and Respiratory Modulation of Autonomic Function, Pain and Health. Am J Pain Manag, 1994; 4(1):36-39.

[xv] Buskila D, Neumann L, Vaisberg G, Alkalay D, Wolfe F. Increased Rates of Fibromyalgia Following Cervical Spine Injury. Arthritis and Rheumatism, 1997; 40(3):446-452.

[xvi] Goodman R, Hypertension and the Atlas Subluxation Complex. J Chiropr Res Clin Investigation, 1992; 8(2):30-32.

[xvii] Cleveland Chiropractic College Website, What is Chiropractic, http://www.clevelandchiropractic.edu/about/about_whatis.htm, 2005.

[xviii] Newman, C, Why Are We So Fat?, National Geographic, Vol. 206 - No.2, page 46, August 2004

[xix] Smiley L, Estimating Your Daily Calorie Requirement, Health Education Online Library, www.health.arizona.edu, 2004.

[xx] Kirschmann J, Dunne L, Nutrition Almanac, II(6), 1984.

[xxi] Statistical Abstract of the United States, Table 204, Page 130, 2001.

[xxii] Owen T, How To Overcome Tired, Irritable & Depressed Feelings, pg. 65, 1979.

[xxiii] Baskin Robbins Website, Nutrition Facts, http://www.baskinrobbins.com/about/nutrition/Product.aspx?Category=Ice%20Cream&id=0658, 2004

[xxiv] Coordinating Committee, Statement from the National High Blood Pressure Education Program, National Institutes of Health, October 14, 1999.

[xxv] Cameron, D, Article - Fresh Living Raw Food vs. Processed Food, http://yourpurelife.com/articles/raw_food.php, March 2006.

[xxvi] Casey, J, The Truth About Fats, WebMDHealth, www.webmd.com, 2005.

[xxvii] Reaves, J, Johnny's New Snack: Milk, Cookies and Prozac, TIME Online Edition, February, 2000.

[xxviii] The Holy Bible, New Living Translation, Romans 7:15, Tyndale House Publishers, 1996

[xxix] Manson, J, A Prospective Study of Walking as Compared with Vigorous Exercise in the Prevention of Coronary Heart Disease in Women, The New England Journal of Medicine, August 1999.

[xxx] Author not identified, www.emedicinehealth.com/articles/42421-2.asp, April 2005.

[xxxi] The Holy Bible, New Living Translation, Matthew 6:27, Tyndale House Publishers, 1996

[xxxii] The Holy Bible, New Living Translation, Ephesians 4:26b, Tyndale House Publishers, 1996

xxxiii Kukula, K, Amazing Facts, www.teacher.scholastic.com, 2005.

xxxiv Nee Watchman, The Spiritual Man, Christian Fellowship Publishers, Inc., New York, pg. 24, 1977.